PARISH PLANNING

PARISH PLANNING

LYLE E. SCHALLER

Nashville • ABINGDON

PARISH PLANNING

Eighth Printing 1980

Copyright © 1971 by Abingdon Press

ISBN 0-687-30102-5
Library of Congress Catalog Card Number: 70-148076

Portions of this book are based on material which
first appeared in periodicals. Grateful acknowledgment is made to the following publications:

The Lutheran, for "Put Your Budget to Work"
(Nov. 8, 1967); "Prescription for Ailing Churches"
(July 15, 1970); "Time to Check the Church
Budget" (Sept. 16, 1970). Copyright 1967 and
1970, Commission on Church Papers, Lutheran
Church in America. Used by permission.

The Interpreter, for "Where Your Treasure Is"
(Nov.-Dec., 1970). Reprinted with permission.

Church Management, for "Marks of a Metropolitan Church" (Sept. 1970).

The Missionary Messenger, for "A New Agenda
for the Small Rural Church" (Mar., 1970).

Religion in Life, for "Redundancy or Efficiency"
(Autumn, 1970), now chap. 8. Copyright © 1970
by Abingdon Press.

MANUFACTURED BY THE PARTHENON PRESS AT
NASHVILLE, TENNESSEE, UNITED STATES OF AMERICA

To
James L. Grazier

ACKNOWLEDGMENTS

In the writing of this volume I have drawn extensively from the experiences, knowledge, wisdom, and insights of others. Most of what is included here is based on what others have said, written, or done. I am especially indebted to the pastors and laymen in the approximately two thousand congregations I have visited during the past decade. I also owe much to the men and women I have worked with in training programs during the past few years and to the ideas, insights, and experiences they have shared so generously.

A special word of gratitude is due the ten men who were with me in a seminar on decision-making and to the ten denominational executives who shared in a workshop on counseling with congregations. Both of these were held in 1970. Verner Carlson, Herb Gosse, Paul Grout, Ted Hulbert, Dowain McKiou, Jim Pender, Curt Rolfe, Nye Bond, Maynard French, John Henderson, Ed Hoefer, Leon Phillips, Mel Schroer, Wayne Selsor, Emmett Streeter, Dick Stolp and Wilbur Whanger will recognize much that is familiar in these pages!

I am also greatly indebted to my colleagues at the Center for Parish Development. Charlotte Wilcox,

Mary Jordan, Bob Gordon, and Dick Tholin have been cooperative, critical in a kindly manner, gracious, thoughtful, and helpful. I am grateful!

This book is dedicated to a man who helped found the Regional Church Planning Office in Cleveland. He was a committed and cheerful Christian, a thoughtful and encouraging friend, and an able and cooperative denominational executive, but I treasure the memory of our association most because he had the warm heart of a pastor.

CONTENTS

INTRODUCTION

The same week in which two men from earth walked on the moon for the first time, a pastors' institute was held at the Lutheran Theological Seminary in Gettysburg, Pennsylvania. Early in one session each minister was asked to suggest a word or phrase that could be used as a synonym for the word "parish" or that expressed a dimension of the life or nature of the parish. Among the suggestions that poured forth were congregation, local church, community, cafeteria, God's love, family, fortress, turtle ("like a mighty turtle"), fellowship, community of believers, people, neighborhood, and covenant.

No one suggested the terms institution, social organization, or voluntary association.

Yet anyone concerned with the life, the work, and the nature of the local church will be able to understand it better if he recognizes that it is both a called out community of believers and a voluntary association in which the right of withdrawal is cherished by many members. He will be more effective in helping to plan the ministry and program of the parish if he can see it as both a covenant and an institution. He will be less surprised and less frustrated by some of the events in the life of the congregation if he can conceive of it as both an expression of God's concern for man and as a social organization.

11

This is a book about the parish (that word is used interchangeably here with the terms local church and congregation), and is not an attempt to define the parish in biblical or theological terms. Rather, it represents an effort to suggest some approaches to parish planning from an institutional perspective.

To a very substantial degree, the typical local church behaves like an institution. A simple illustration of this is that in most congregations, as in other institutions in our society, the first claim on the resources of money and manpower is for essential institutional maintenance—and the definition of "essential" changes with the quantity of resources available. Therefore, the basic central assumption in this book is that the person interested in planning for the life, mission, and future of the parish can benefit by recognizing the fact that the local church is a social organization.

Furthermore, since on many occasions the parish behaves like other institutions, the local church leader can benefit by the knowledge and wisdom that has been accumulated in other disciplines about organizational behavior. A book such as *Innovation in Marketing* by Theodore Levitt deservedly won a national award as an outstanding contribution to the literature in the field of marketing. In addition, however, because it contains a tremendous amount of wisdom about the relationships of both the leadership and the clientele to an organization, it also has much to say to the leaders in the local church. In the suggestions for further reading at the end of each chapter, several books and articles from the administrative and behavioral sciences have been listed. While some may respond, as one denominational executive did,

12

to a similar list—"These don't have anything to do with the church"—it is hoped that others may find useful insights, suggestions, and ideas in these publications.

One of the major contributions from these other disciplines has been to a redefinition of the concept of planning. Twenty years ago the typical person bearing the professional label of "planner" had received his academic training in architecture, engineering, or landscape architecture; he probably was employed by a city planning commission and almost invariably was concerned primarily, and often exclusively, with the orderly physical growth of the city. He was expected to prepare a "master plan" that was focused largely or entirely on the use of land. The zoning ordinance, subdivision regulations, capital improvements program, and urban redevelopment were viewed as the basic tools for implementing the master plan.

Today only a relatively few of the professional planners under thirty-five have been trained in physical design, a very large proportion are employed in business, industry, the federal government, in both public and private social agencies, and by a rapidly growing number of consulting firms. Today the emphasis is not on producing a plan, but on the process of defining purpose, formulating goals, and translating ideas into programs. Today the responsibility of the typical planner has been changed from producing a plan to improving the decision-making process in the organization. Today the planner who is functioning within a contemporary definition of the word planning is basically concerned with two questions—goal formulation and policy development.

It is within this context of this contemporary recognition of the importance of goals and policies that this book has been written. The purpose of this volume is not to provide an instruction manual for the congregation that wants to prepare a plan for that local church for 1985. The purpose of this book is to offer some suggestions and guidance on how the people in a local church can improve the quality of the decision-making process in that parish as they seek to respond in faithfulness and obedience to the call of the Lord to that band of pilgrims. The "product" of that process will vary from congregation to congregation. In one parish it may be in the form of a budget, in another it may be a series of policy guidelines, in a third it may be a set of action proposals, in another it may be a statement of goals, in a fourth it may be a single proposal for a new ministry, and in another it may be simply a one-sheet redefinition of the statement of purpose of that particular parish. In each case, however, it is hoped that product will be concerned, in one form or another, with the central issues of goals and policies. There is no single right answer to the question, "What should be in a final report of our parish planning committee?" Hopefully, no such committee will seek to prepare a *final* report.

This leads to one final comment about the contemporary definition of planning. A great many planning committees have sought to produce a final report that would be a permanent guide for decades. In the 1950's and even in the 1960's, for example, there were published reports carrying the label "A Plan for X City for 1980" or "A Plan for X Congregation for 1975." Many of these plans were based on the apparent assumption that never again would there

14

be gathered together a group of people with the wisdom, the vision, the knowledge, and the divine inspiration that was represented in that planning committee. Therefore, that committee had an obligation to make as many irrevocable decisions affecting the future as possible. Better to make a few minor errors than to leave any of these decisions to the people who would be in charge twenty years hence!

More recently, there has emerged a concept that is sometimes referred to as non-planning. This is based on the assumption that the leaders of tomorrow not only may not be stupid, it is possible they will have greater wisdom, more reliable knowledge, and keener insights than are possessed by today's leaders. While such an assumption is difficult for some of us to accept, it does lead to a very important comment about the responsibilities of today's planning committee. Every recommendation and every decision should be made in the context of this question. Will this enlarge or reduce the alternatives open to the decision-makers in this organization fifteen and twenty years from now? The distinctive emphasis in non-planning is to maximize the number of options kept open for future decision-makers in the organization.

While this book has been written to serve as a resource for parish leaders and to stand on its own merits, in one sense it is a sequel to *The Local Church Looks to the Future*. That book emphasized the importance of a definition of purpose, suggested that differences in the definition of purpose constitute the greatest single source of tension in the churches, and included chapters on specific parish planning problems such as interchurch cooperation, building planning, and evangelism.

In this volume the central emphasis is on finding

15

the "handles" for beginning the planning process, on the critical importance of self-evaluation, and on the implementation process or turning ideas and plans into program and ministry. Those who want an introduction into the church planning process, who seek more guidance on developing a statement of purpose, who have some questions about the value of the goal formation process, who seek more detail on some of the specific questions mentioned in the previous paragraph, or who would like an elaboration of the process of planned social change, may want to turn to *The Local Church Looks to the Future* either before or after reading this volume.

While the relationship of the chapters in this volume represents what appears to be a logical sequence to at least one person, each has been planned and written to stand alone. For example, the person who wants to read only about the implementation process can turn directly to chapter 5 without fear of encountering passages that presume an acquaintanceship with material in an earlier chapter. Scattered through the book are references to major blocs of related material in other chapters.

Those persons who prefer to start at the beginning and read straight through a book in the fashion the Lord, and all respectable publishers, intended a book to be read, deserve the courtesy of a road map. In this book the journey starts with a pilgrimage or, to be more precise, with the suggestion that the analogies of a covenant and a pilgrimage provide a helpful frame of reference for parish planning. The idea of a four-way covenant offers an easy approach to developing an operational definition of purpose. The image of a band of pilgrims strung out along the road suggests some of the questions on purpose, goals, per-

16

spective, communication, and participation that should be recognized in the parish planning process, and especially by those who strongly desire rapid, radical change.

Perhaps the most frequently raised "practical" question on the subject of parish planning is "Where do we begin?" In many respects, one of the best answers to that question is the budget and this is discussed in chapter 2.

The most subversive force in the local church today is institutional blight. It is also the biggest obstacle to effective planning. The nature and form of this problem and two suggestions for responses to institutional blight constitute chapter 3. The most effective approach to the problem of institutional blight in any organization is to build in a process of continuing self-evaluation based on the definition of purpose, and also to establish lines of accountability. The critical nature of evaluation and accountability, together with specific suggestions on how to do it can be found in chapter 4. Some readers may conclude this is the most useful section of the book.

There is a growing body of opinion in the business world, in political circles, and in several places in the churches that the most urgent need today is not for new ideas, but rather for an increased capability in implementing ideas, plans, and programs that already exist. This point of view is reflected in the comparatively lengthy fifth chapter where several dimensions of the implementation process are analyzed and discussed.

With the relatively rapid disappearance of the geographical parish from the American church scene it often is useful to look at types of churches in developing a relevant frame of reference for parish planning. Some of the values of this concept are suggested in chapter 6, and these are followed by an analysis of some of the questions before four different types of congregations today. These four types were chosen partly to illustrate how the concept of looking at churches by types can be useful, and partly because each of the four types described is faced with severe tension-producing questions and problems.

In far too many congregations, evangelism has been neglected as the leaders place a greater emphasis in planning for real estate development, finances, worship, and education. Chapter 7 represents a relatively brief attempt to suggest some approaches that have proved helpful in other congregations.

Increasingly, today, the emphasis in our society is on improving the quality of performance. This is in contrast to the traditional emphasis on economy and efficiency. One approach to this issue has been largely overlooked in the churches, but is a standard operating principle in many other fields of endeavor. This is discussed in the final chapter, with some suggestions for adapting the theory of redundancy to church planning. Hopefully the person who reads this chapter last will be more understanding of the repetition that he encountered in the first seven chapters.

1
THE COVENANT AND
THE PILGRIMAGE

"You're asking what is the source of the problems facing this parish? That's an easy question! There is no doubt but that all of our problems here at St. Timothy's grew out of the fact that most of our members don't take their membership vows seriously. They seem to have forgotten that when they became members of this congregation they promised to support the church by their prayers, their presence, their service, and their gifts."

The layman who gave this response to a question from a visiting church planner was identifying a situation that can be found in more than a few parishes. Too many church members do not take their membership vows seriously. It is difficult to resolve this problem, however, without first looking at all facets of the relationship between the individual church member and the congregation.

When an individual joins a local church, whether by believer's baptism, profession of faith, confirmation, or by transfer from another congregation, he enters into what could be described as a four-way covenant. One dimension of this covenant is between the individual and God. A second is between the new member and the other members as individuals as they agree to bear one another's burdens and to minister to one another in the name of Jesus Christ.

A third element of this covenant, and the one referred to in the earlier paragraph, is the set of obligations the new member assumes when he joins that institution known as a local church. While it is true that the parish is only an institutional expression of the universal church, for most Christians it is the primary relationship between himself and the Christian church. Most church members feel only a very limited relationship to the denomination and an even more limited tie to the regional judicatory such as the synod, district, conference, association, convention, or diocese.

In addition, it should not be forgotten that all other institutional expressions of the church, such as a council of churches, a denomination, a chaplaincy, a seminary, and the whole array of specialized ministries are largely or entirely dependent upon the parish. Without the local church they could not, or at least probably would not, exist. Thus the loyalty of the individual church member to the congregation to which he belongs is a matter of grave importance to all who believe in the validity and the importance of the Christian church in its many institutional forms.

There is a fourth dimension to the covenant, however, that is often neglected. This is the obligation of the congregation as a whole, as a parish, to the member. This is different from the covenant between the new member and the other individuals who are members of that congregation. That is a person-to-person relationship. This is the relationship between the parish as an institution and the individual.

What Does the Parish Owe the Members?

In looking at this part of the covenant which covers the obligations of the congregation to the member, five elements merit consideration by the members of the parish planning committee.

The first, and most obvious, is the obligation of the local church to minister to the member in the traditional patterns. This includes providing opportunities for corporate worship; offering a ministry of concern and care in time of illness, pain, sorrow and suffering; celebrating occasions of joy and happiness, such as the birth of a baby, a baptism or a wedding; and sponsoring a range of fellowship activities.

A second obligation, and one that is seldom mentioned, is the responsibility to the older person who may have been a member of that congregation for fifty or sixty or seventy years. Too often this obligation is lightly dismissed and a congregation dissolves or relocates without helping this elderly member find a new church home and be assimilated into a new Christian fellowship.

Perhaps the obligation that has been receiving the most attention in recent years has been the responsibility of the local church to provide for the members a variety of opportunities for personal and spiritual growth. The growth of the small group concept, the work of the Ecumenical Institute, the spread of the Yokefellow movement, the increasing popularity of the weekend retreat, the rapidly expanding opportunities for lay training seminars and the tremendous growth in weekday programs of Christian education for adults are examples of how the churches have been recognizing and responding to this obligation. Other illustrations are the congregation in West

21

Virginia that sends a different member on a round-the-world tour of the mission field each year, and the Nebraska synod that arranged charter flights to visit the mission work in Latin America.

Perhaps more significant than the expansion of study opportunities has been the somewhat belated recognition that study without response or challenge without commitment is both psychologically wrong and spiritually stultifying. This brings up the fourth obligation of the local church to its members. This is the obligation of every parish to provide a range and variety of opportunities to be involved in ministry. As a result, in hundreds of local churches today, laymen are being offered both the possibility for personal and spiritual growth *and* the opportunity for personal witness and service. These opportunities for ministry range from preaching to picketing, from serving as president of the men's club to seeing America through the eyes of a black person, from calling on shut-ins to tutoring high school drop-outs, from serving as parish treasurer to raising the bail money for a group of Black Panthers, from counseling the youth fellowship to serving as a community organizer, and from painting the parsonage to manning a first aid tent at a rock festival.

A fifth, and perhaps the most neglected of the obligations of the local church to its members, is to treat each member as a person. In this object-oriented society it is easy to drift into an attitude in which church members are perceived as numbers or cases or cards or things rather than as children of God.

When a local church begins to view members as objects or numbers, the members tend to respond with the same degree of animation and enthusiasm that is expressed by an object such as a book or a pew or a three-by-five card. When the pastor and the lay leaders act as though they believe each member has feelings and can be hurt by a careless word or a thoughtless deed or inspired by an act of concern or a thoughtful word, the members tend to respond with the animation and enthusiasm that is a characteristic of a member of the called-out community.

A very important dimension of this fifth obligation of the parish to the member is the opportunity his church offers him to commit himself to meaningful goals and worthwhile challenges. The fundamental commitment, of course, is to Jesus Christ as Lord and Savior. Too often, however, this is the only commitment asked of the member and the only opportunity he is offered to make a commitment. Faith without works is dead, and there are too many congregations that have demanded of the members a purity of faith but never opened the door for a response by the members to that faith. To pick up a concept that is elaborated on in chapter 5, a statement of goals can be in a generalized form that sounds impressive but does not have any handles for beginning the implementation process. Likewise, the call to commitment can be in either generalized terms or in *operational* terms that enables the one who is being called to understand not only what is being asked, but also challenges him with a clearly defined opportunity for a response. Perhaps a more straightforward statement would be to say the local church has an obligation to the members to translate the usual pious platitudes into terms and challenges an ordinary human being can understand. The language of the parish should be a language that helps, rather than inhibits, the movement of people as they go from where they are to where God calls them to be.

This same concept of moving from here to there is a basic element of the church planning process. Repeatedly both laymen and pastors turn to the church planner with the problem, "We want some help, first in deciding what this parish should be five years from now and second, in figuring out how we get from here to there."

Is that trip from here to there a parade or a pilgrimage?

Parade or Pilgrimage?

Some congregations do resemble a poorly organized parade. All the people, cars, floats, bands, and other components have been standing in the hot July sun for an hour waiting for the parade to begin. No one is quite sure of the exact route or where they are supposed to go after passing the reviewing stand. Eventually a few units start out and now it is possible to identify the leaders without any question, but only a few relatives among the spectators along the curb can draw the line precisely between the last of the marchers, who were part of the formal parade when it began, and the energetic cyclists, the enthusiastic children, and the impatient motorists who mixed in with the stragglers when they made a wrong turn two blocks before reaching the reviewing stand.

Other congregations resemble one of the marching bands in the parade. They convey the impression that they know without any doubt or reservation who they are, where they are going, and what they will do when they get there. There is no question who is a member and who is not a member of the group. The members depend upon their leader for instruction and direction. They respond to his commands with a sense of obedience and discipline that greatly

24

impresses the spectators. It is clear, however, that most people would rather stand and watch than to join that group with its authoritarian leadership and demanding standards for membership.

Most Christian congregations in the United States, however, probably can be described more meaningfully in symbolic terms as a column of pilgrims rather than by use of the analogy of the parade.

This pilgrimage consists of a long line of people extending perhaps a mile or more down the road. They are not marching in a single file column, but rather are clustered in groups of varying size. The careful observer notes that this actually is not a pilgrimage of, say four to five hundred individuals, but is really a column composed of perhaps twenty or thirty or forty clusters with many people moving back and forth and being members of several different clusters in the same column.

This observer also sees that as the pilgrimage moves down the road many people drop out, some for a brief rest on the grassy bank beside the road, others turn off at an intersection and join another column, and quite a few simply seem to disappear. He also observes that as the pilgrimage moves along the pace varies, the leadership shifts, and occasionally even the direction changes. He sees this column of pilgrims pause briefly every once in a while to bury a member, or to welcome new pilgrims into the pilgrimage, but the pilgrimage always keeps moving. At times, however, this observer has to set a couple of stakes in the ground to determine in which direction some of the columns are going.

The observer also notes that occasionally one of these columns of pilgrims simply disappears. Ten miles back it was there as a very distinctive separate column. Now it is gone. Some of the familiar faces can be seen in other columns, but many have simply disappeared.

The longer he watches and the more columns of pilgrims this observer sees as they go marching past his vantage point, the more he is impressed by the tremendous variety. He sees columns go by that clearly know where they have been, where they are going, and where they are now. He remembers the definition of the psychologically healthy person as the individual who is linked to the past, is convinced he can influence the future, and is able and happy to live in the present. Perhaps this is also a definition of a healthy column of pilgrims.

He also is tremendously impressed by those occasional columns that, as they go marching by, are clearly more than just columns—each one is really a community, a community of interdependent people and groups in which the themes of hope, celebration, and servanthood stand out.

As this observer watches literally hundreds and hundreds of columns of pilgrims go marching down the road past his vantage point, he is baffled by an apparent contradiction. As he looks out, he can see anywhere from a half dozen to perhaps a hundred separate columns going by at any one time, some so close it is almost impossible to distinguish one column from another. Yet it appears that the vast majority of these columns of pilgrims are marching along on the apparent assumption that there is not another column on the road for several miles in either direction!

As he watches, he observes many other interesting sights. He sees one column that is marching without a map and every time it comes to a fork in the road, it never stops to look at the road signs, but always automatically selects the smoothest and easiest path. As he watches, he sees that it never chooses a road leading up a hill nor a path that is filled with rocks and other obstacles. Apparently it is more concerned with the trip than with the destination.

He also sees what appears to be a growing number of columns with road maps. They appear to know where they are going, and whenever these columns reach a fork in the road, they make a choice, apparently not on the basis of the attractiveness of the road, but rather on the basis of reaching a predetermined destination.

As he watches, he is interested in the appeal the different columns make to those persons sitting on the tree-lined bank beside the road. Some of these are individuals who had dropped out of columns that had passed by earlier, and some apparently had never been a part of any pilgrimage. He sees one column go by heavily burdened with a tremendous load of baggage. As they struggle along, they call out to those sitting by the road to come join them, but very few get up. He sees another column, unencumbered by so many bags, trunks, and suitcases, which appears to be moving rather rapidly. Different individuals and small groups from this column regularly hand their bags over to be carried by another member while they hurry over to the side of the road to help some of the people who appear to be in pain or experiencing difficulties. While the observer never hears anyone from that column ask people to join them, he is impressed by the number of persons who have been sitting by the side of the road watching, suddenly get up and on their own initiative join this column.

As he watches these columns of pilgrims go marching past, the observer realizes that what he is seeing is the view from one comparatively isolated vantage point along the road. As he sits there making notes on what he sees and hears, he wonders what others are seeing from other perspectives and from other observation points in both directions along the road.

The Covenant

When a group of people covenant to take a journey together, the covenant becomes a controlling factor throughout the journey. The Mayflower Compact was an example of this in early American history. So it is in the local church. When a person joins a Christian congregation, he is entering into a covenant which not only sets out the style of life for the pilgrimage, it also sets out the measurements for evaluating what happens on that pilgrimage. Therefore, when the members of a congregation enter into a covenant to take a pilgrimage together down life's road, they should ask themselves if the covenant provides not only for all four of the elements identified in the covenant described at the beginning of this chapter, but they also should ask if it provides for a means of determining how effectively all four elements of the covenant are being observed. It is questionable whether any congregation can act with integrity in its relationships with both its members and with the total community unless it has a sense of being a covenant community.

The congregation that perceives itself as a covenant community has valuable insight as it begins to plan for mission. While the dominant emphasis in succeeding chapters is on the local church as a voluntary association, it is more than that. It is first of all a covenant community. The congregation that recognizes this has an effective counterforce for the inevitable pressures of institutionalism that are a part of the decision-making process in any voluntary association.

Likewise, the congregation that can perceive its life and mission as a pilgrimage also has an analogy that can yield valuable insights into the parish planning process. It may help to suggest a few of these. Some are simple, a few are more complex, but all can be helpful as background.

The ancient expression, "The longest journey begins with a single step," applies to the concept of a pilgrimage and to the congregation that is asking, "How do we get into mission?"

Relatively few persons in today's congregations were members when that local church first began its pilgrimage. Most people join the pilgrimage after it is already under way. It has identified a direction and set its pace. Any changes from the status quo are changes in an already established direction and an already accepted pace. Few congregations that decide to begin planning seriously for mission are starting with a blank slate. A few may be simply walking around in a circle, but they already have been some place and they are moving. Therefore, any planning for tomorrow must begin with an identification of the point where that column of pilgrims is today, which way it is headed, the pace at which it is moving, and the procedures that have been used for making a decision when it reached a fork in the road.

Like the columns of pilgrims described earlier, most local churches tend to be separate, self-governing, autonomous, and independent organizations. Denominational labels tend to obscure the fact

29

that every local church that can and does pay its bills is congregational in terms of church government. The closest there is to an exception to that generalization is the United Presbyterian Church in the U.S.A.— and many northern Presbyterians will laugh when they read that!

This strong sense of congregational autonomy that runs all through American Protestantism (and increasingly through all of the Christian religious groups in the United States) is an extremely important factor in parish planning. It is important partly because it tends to be overlooked and partly because it is increasingly difficult for any congregation to implement its plans for mission and ministry effectively on a unilateral basis. Yet there is a strong tendency for each band of pilgrims to assume it is the only column on that road.

There is also a tendency for each group of pilgrims to act on the assumption that it not only is the only column on that road, but that it is the *first* column to ever go down that particular road. Occasionally this is true. The reality of the scene for most congregations, however, is that they are neither alone nor are they pioneers. They can learn much from others.

When this tendency toward isolation is combined with the fact that the most distinctive characteristic of American Protestantism is the churches' ability to keep secret nearly all of the truly outstanding examples of effective and meaningful ministry, it is easy to see why every congregation feels constrained to re-invent the wheel.

The obvious implication is that the congregation that is seriously interested in planning for its mission can develop a more effective planning process by exploiting the resources and experiences of others.

This is easier said than done in a day when the climate for church planning has been clouded by a combination of anti-intellectualism, antidenominationalism, and anti-institutionalism. This possibility of benefittng from the experiences of others also has been inhibited by the adoption by many religious magazines of that old expression of the secular press that "Bad news is better news than good news."

Learning from Others

For the congregation that seeks to benefit from the experiences and the accumulated knowledge and wisdom of others, there are several places to turn.

The first place to turn is the Bible. Here is found not only the Word of God, but also a record of accumulated wisdom about man, his behavior, and his relationships to institutions. Here also are found in the New Testament instructive statements on the nature and purpose of the church. In his letters to the early churches, Paul wrote what could be described as the first book on church planning.

A second place to turn is the denomination. Denominational staff members not only can serve as consultants to the local church, they can bring to bear the experiences of other congregations.

More important than this consultative role, however, is for the people in the parish to see the denominational judicatory as a partner in ministry. There are many tasks before the churches today that cannot be performed by individual congregations or even by clusters of congregations. If these ministries are to be carried out, they must be accomplished by the denominations. Some of these are obvious, such as the education of clergymen, the preparation of materials for Christian education, and camping programs. In addition to these, however, there is a growing challenge in the area of witness and mission that will not be met unless there is a response by and through the denominational judicatory. Unfortunately, the voice of a Harvey Cox, who pleads with committed Christian laymen to avoid involvement in the denominational bureaucracy, receives a wider hearing than Presbyterian Richard Moore or Episcopalian Paul Moore. Every behavioral scientist recognizes that in a society dominated by institutions the only possibility for religion to be influential is through some institutionalized expression of religion.

Today when the local church is stronger and more vital than it has been for decades, when the Christian faith is having a greater impact on American society than it has had for at least fifty years, and when the value system of Christianity is attracting more adherents than every before in this century, the darkest cloud on the horizon may be that coalition of "radical renewalists" and extremely conservative churchmen who would still the prophetic witness and the social ministry of the church by wiping out all institutional expressions of the church beyond the parish.

A third place to turn in planning for mission is to other congregations. Here again there are two questions each congregation can ask with profit. They are basically the same questions that should be asked of the denominational judicatory. "What can we learn from your experiences?" "What can we do together in mission and ministry more effectively than we can do alone?"

A fourth place for parish leaders to turn for help as they begin to plan for the future ministry of their parish is to the knowledge and wisdom that has been accumulated in business administration, public administration, and the behavioral sciences. An effort has been made to incorporate some of these resources into the remaining chapters of this volume.

Opportunities, Visions, and Style

The congregation that can visualize itself as a column of pilgrims can see that as this band of travelers moves down the road they are certain to encounter a changing environment, varying opportunities, and new challenges. This is also true in the local church and can be illustrated by two examples.

In most denominations the women's organization in the local church is encountering increasing difficulties. One reason is the erosion of the original purpose. A second reason is the changing role of women in American society. The status-quo-oriented person will seek to restore the women's organization to its former place of strength and influence. The pilgrim will recognize this is a different point on the road and look forward to a redefinition of purpose and to redefining the functions of the women's organization in terms of the new circumstances and the new role of women. The pilgrim will recognize the local church has to provide equal opportunities for women, it has to offer new challenges and it has to provide a new array of training opportunities. (Those who are offended by this illustration may substitute the phrase youth fellowship for women's organization and the word teen-agers for women in the above paragraph.)

A second example is the Sunday school which is in even worse institutional difficulties than either the women's organization or the youth fellowship. The status-quo-oriented person will try to restore the Sunday school to its former glory. The pilgrim will look back and see how at one stretch of the road, beginning nearly two hundred years ago, the Sunday school was a tremendously relevant and helpful response to an urgent need. He will now look at where he is on the road to see the needs which can be met by new methods and forms of Christian education.

The pilgrim is motivated to keep moving down what appears to be an endless road by a vision before him. Without that vision, sooner or later, he will succumb to the temptation to go over and sit in the shade and rest his weary bones. Once he does, unless he perceives a new vision, he is unlikely ever to move out of the shade. An excellent illustration of the operational use of this concept is the experience of Centenary United Methodist Church in Winston-Salem, North Carolina. This congregation conceived a vision of what their church should be in the future. They outlined this in a booklet called "Centenary's Vision in a Changing World." This booklet was in two sections. The first described the program and ministry as it existed; the second was the vision of what could be. This brought the vision before the entire congregation. A year later they reprinted the booklet and added a third section in which they reported what had been accomplished thus far in turning the vision into reality, but they also held out what remained to be done. Through this method of communication, that local church set before the membership a vision of what could be and also conveyed a sense of movement, progress, and achievement.

Finally, the use of the pilgrim analogy provides a useful frame of reference for examining the life style of a congregation. In a remarkable book that deserves the careful scrutiny of anyone concerned with the

ministry and future of the local church, Gerald J.
Jud outlines the pilgrim style of congregational life.
Among the characteristics he lifts up are faith and
hope; an acceptance of the concept of living for
others; openness to the future; belief in a God of
creation, a God who loves the world, a God who hates
bondage, and a God who covenants with us.

Now where does the congregation that is a covenant
community, a band of pilgrims, and also a voluntary
association begin the parish planning process?

SUGGESTIONS FOR FURTHER READING

Barr, Browne. *Parish Back Talk*. Nashville: Abingdon
Press, 1964.

Clark, M. Edward; Malcomson, William L.; and
Molton, Warren Lane. *The Church Creative*. Nashville: Abingdon Press, 1967.

Cox, Harvey. *The Secular City*. New York: The Macmillan Co., 1965.

Gans, Herbert J. "From Urbanism to Policy-Making,"
Journal of the American Institute of Planners. July,
1970.

Jud, Gerald J. *Pilgrim's Process*. Philadelphia:
United Church Press, 1967.

Moore, Paul, Jr. *The Church Reclaims the City*. New
York: Seabury Press, 1964.

Moore, Richard E. and Day, Duane L. *Urban
Church Breakthrough*. New York: Harper and
Row, 1966.

Moore, Richard E. "The Missionary Structure of the
United Presbyterian Church," *McCormick Quar-
terly*, March, 1966.

Whitley, Oliver Read. *The Church: Mirror or Win-
dow?* St. Louis: Bethany Press, 1969.

2
THE EASIEST PLACE
TO BEGIN

"I don't know whether it is my own shortcomings or whether it is the churches I have been serving," remarked a forty-year-old minister in his third pastorate, "but I never have been able to get more than a handful of people in the congregation to talk seriously about the purpose and mission of the church or to show any interest in planning for the future of the parish.

"Everywhere I go I hear about the urgent need to emphasize purpose and to plan, and I know some parishes have done a good job at this, but frankly I am at a loss about where to begin. The folks in this congregation who will come out for a Bible study group are not the ones who make the decisions, and the people who make the decisions simply aren't interested in spending six Tuesday nights studying the New Testament definition of the church.

"What I need," he concluded, "is some practical advice on how I can help the leaders in my congregation find some handles to begin this process of planning for the mission of this parish!"

There are at least three approaches to this pastor's dilemma.

Theoretically the best approach, but for him apparently the least practical, is to begin with the New Testament definition of the church and to move from that point to the development of a statement of purpose for that congregation, the development of a series of policy guidelines, and the formulation of long-term goals and short-range objectives. A very small but increasing number of congregations are following this sequence.

The most common beginning point is a problem or crisis. A great many congregations do not begin to give any serious thought to purpose or mission, or talk about planning for the future, until a problem or crisis forces them to do so. The cause of this new concern about purpose and the future may be declining attendance, an overcrowded church school, a changing neighborhood, a fire, a highway project that will take part of the church property, a denominational merger, the resignation, death, or retirement of the pastor, the opportunity to purchase the house next door to the church, an urban renewal project, or any of a dozen similar events.

The *easiest* point in many congregations is to begin with the parish budget. This is not to suggest this is the best or the only place for a congregation to begin the process of meaningful discussions about purpose, mission, policies, and goals, but it is the easiest.

There are several reasons why this is true. First, nearly every congregation in the mainline Protestant denominations depends on an annual budget in the administration of the parish. Second, usually a group of laymen share most or all of the responsibility for the preparation of the budget. Third, many members of most parishes have relevant useful personal experiences in the preparation and use of a budget. Tens of thousands of congregations have professional budget officers or financial experts in the membership. Fourth, the budget is one document that attracts the interest of most parish leaders. Fifth, the budget can be a very versatile document. This can be seen more clearly by asking the question, what is a budget?

What Is a Budget?

The budget of the local church or of the conference or of a synod or of a diocese or of a family or of a nation may be a mass of numbers summarized on one sheet of paper.

It also can be far more than that. It can be an extraordinarily helpful tool in the decision-making process. A budget can be many things, including the following.

1. *A Theological Document*

It is a theological document. It identifies the gods that are worshiped in that organization and the ranking of those gods in that organization's hierarchy.

For example, the budget of the federal government for 1970–71 included these expenditures:

National defense .... $68.6 billion
Farm subsidies .... 5.4 billion
Space exploration .... 3.8 billion
Air and highway travel ...... 2.7 billion
Housing for low income
    families .... 0.4 billion

To some, this suggests the ranking of the gods worshiped by the American people.

In the regional judicatory of one denomination, the annual budget allocations could be described by these percentages.

Forwarded to the national church .. 51%
Regional denominational
    programming 6%
Grants to hospitals, homes, and
    colleges 37%
Helping local churches fulfill their
    ministry 6%

In one congregation the annual expenditures were divided into three categories.

A ministry to the membership 80.1%
Evangelism and outreach 0.3%
Witness and mission in the community, in the state, in the nation, and in the world 19.6%

Does the budget in your congregation represent your theology?

2. A *Statement of Purpose*
    The budget can be read as a statement of purpose. The careful reader can study the priorities reflected by the allocation of resources and thus perceive the purposes of the organization.

    Just as a poem can be translated from French into English and then back into French, a budget represents the translation of purpose into financial terms. The financial statement can be translated back into a definition of purpose. Occasionally some of the original intent and meaning is lost in the process of translation.

3. A *Political Document*
    It is a political document. Politics concerns the allocation of scarce resources, and the budget

records the allocation of that organization's financial resources.

As a political document, the budget frequently is a record of the resolution of conflicts. These include the conflict about the definition of purpose, the conflict over goals, the conflict about priorities, the conflict between needs and resources, the conflict between new demands and established precedents, and the conflict between the dream and the possible.

4. *A Box Score*

The budget often can be viewed as the box score recording the winners and the losers and the achievements of each. It records all winners and most, but not all, losers. The loser who is defeated 4–3 appears in the budget box score, but the loser who is shut out in his first appearance, whether it be 1 or 0 or 17 to 0, rarely is mentioned in the budget.

It may provide the "winners" with the sense of accomplishment, approval from peers or superiors, and the satisfaction that builds an inner sense of commitment, loyalty, and accomplishment. It also may encourage within the "losers" a feeling of dissatisfaction, reduced commitment and diminished loyalty to the organization.

5. *A Diagram of Expectations*

The budget is a future-oriented document (the better the budgeting process the greater the emphasis on the future). It is a statement of what the organization expects to buy and the sources from which it expects to receive the resources necessary to purchase these items. In terms of expectations, budgets range between a dream at one end of the continuum and a contract at the other extreme.

Traditionally, budgets have tended to have a strong orientation to the past. The budgets of most ecclesiastical organizations appear to have been prepared on the assumption the world will come to an end a year from next December 31. For example, in the 1972 budget both the receipts and expenditures sections may have these columns:

1968	1969	1970	1971	1972
actual	actual	actual	estimated request	adopted

In such a format, a future orientation can be developed by adding these additional columns:

1973	1974	1975	1976
proposed	proposed	proposed	proposed

This will encourage those preparing the 1972 budget request to plan ahead for future years. It will enable those charged with the responsibility of preparing the total organizational budget to consider the future expectations of each agency and group within the organization.

A second method of developing a stronger future orientation in the organization through the budgetary process is to ask, "What proportion of current and proposed expenditures are for financing current program activities, and what proportion are for increasing the future capability of the organization to accomplish its purpose and fulfill its mission?". The expenditures for janitorial services in a building or for rent would be in the first category, while a training program might be in the second category.

6. *A Plan*

A budget can be a statement of expectations; it also can be a plan that specifies goals, places a price tag on each goal, and includes a strategy for achieving these goals. As a plan, the budget is a link between today's understanding of reality and the hopes for tomorrow. It is a strategy for moving the organization from where it is to where currently it is believed that it ought to be.

7. *A Communications Network*

The budget does serve as a channel of communication linking one segment of the organization to another (such as the finance committee and the membership of the group).

It also can be a communications network linking together the various groups and programs of the organization. As the budget preparation process unfolds and as the budget is implemented information is being generated and fed into this communication network from many sources.

The quality of the budgeting process controls the quality of this communications network. This is a striking example of the relevance of the computer term GIGO (garbage in, garbage out). Does your budget as it is presented to the membership enlighten or confuse? Does it improve or impede the transmission of information within the organization? Or, to put it another way, the basic question is not "Is your budget a channel of communication in your church?" The budget *is* a channel of communication. Therefore, the question that should be asked is "What messages are you communicating via this channel?"

8. A *Basis for Evaluation*
    The budget can be used as a basis for evaluating
    the performance of the organization; for compar-
    ing the purpose and the expectations with the
    actual performance; for a periodic report of prog-
    ress and for comparing input with output. This
    can be illustrated by a simple example.
    Every local church budget should include these
    two lines:
    "Continuing education for the
        pastor .... $???"
    "Inservice training for laymen .... $???"
    One reason for including these in the budget is
    to provide the necessary financing. Another rea-
    son is that placing them in the budget calls
    attention to these needs and thus provides a
    highly visible reminder. In effect, the report of
    the treasurer each month provides one means of
    evaluating progress in responding to these two
    needs as performance is compared with prior
    expectations.
    The budget also can be used as a lever to
    encourage self-evaluation and also an outside
    evaluation of agencies and groups within the
    organization. Some organizations require an
    evaluation of the current program to be a part
    of the request for funds for the coming year.
    The more clearly the purpose, the long-term
    goals, and the short-term objectives of the
    organization are expressed in the budget, the
    more useful is the budget in the evaluation
    process.

9. A *Precedent*
    Once adopted, a budget becomes a precedent
    for future decisions. It is more difficult to subtract

43

an existing category of expenditures than it is to add a new program in the budget. Normally, only major departures from previous patterns are subjected to close scrutiny in the budget preparation process.

The importance of precedent is best illustrated by the proponents of a new program who often are as much concerned about "getting into the budget" as with the dollar amount allocated to the new program in the budget.

A useful method for breaking the power of precedent is to establish a percentage distribution basis for the allocation of funds that reflects the purpose and the goals of the organization *before* the actual detailed budget preparation process is begun.

A second approach is "zero budgeting." Instead of using last year's budget as a basis for preparing the new budget for the coming year, place a zero opposite each item that was in the previous year's budget. Instead of assuming last year's figure is appropriate unless proved otherwise, assume a zero is the appropriate figure unless proved otherwise. One large congregation in Florida adopted the zero budgeting procedure and in the first year of this practice fourteen items that "always had been included in the budget" were dropped completely.

A third means of combating the power of precedent is to require a reduction (typically ten or fifteen percent) in the total amount that can be allocated to items that were in last year's budget. A reversal of this approach is to reserve ten or fifteen percent of the total funds available for new work, new ministries, and new projects.

10. *An Administrative Instrument*

One of the most important characteristics of the budgetary process is that it prevents indefinite procrastination, creates deadlines, demands decisions, and largely eliminates equivocation. The budget is an instrument for controlling expenditures; it serves as a basis for accountability in expenditures and often imposes a set of mutual obligations on the participants in the organization. It can be a means for coordinating both planning and programming.

The budget often sets both a floor and a ceiling for receipts. This informal "control" is both a reflection of expectations and a creator of expectations.

The value of the budget as an administrative instrument can be enhanced by the use of the "performance budget or "program budget" format or by the use of the Planning–Programming–Budgeting System (PPBS). (PPBS is discussed in more detail in a subsequent section of this chapter.) Each of these uses the budget as a part of the planning process and lifts up both "input" and "output" sides of the budget. The program budget is especially helpful, since it not only forces consideration of unit costs, it also places the emphasis on ministry rather than pledges.

11. *A Focus for Alienation*

The decisions on the allocation of the resources that are represented in the budget may be a cause of alienation among those who disagree most strongly with the purposes and goals expressed by those decisions.

The budget also may be a focal point for the

application of sanctions—both by those contributing to the receipts side of the budget and by those controlling the expenditures side.

12. A *Rallying Point*

The strength of economic pressures in American society means that the budget can be the rallying point for those who have questions and concerns about the purpose, role, structure, and future of the organization.

This may be the point at which the budget represents the greatest unrealized potential for those congregations seeking an effective beginning point in the planning process. If the discussion about the budget can be shifted from money to ministry, from economy to effectiveness, and from means to purpose, there may be no ceiling on what Christians will do to fulfill their calling.

Input or Output?

A growing number of churches have discovered that preparing the budget is a valuable way of identifying their fundamental objectives and of determining how well they are meeting them.

They do this with methods which have been used successfully in government and industry for several years, and which are now finding their way into church administration. One is called *performance* budgeting; the other is known as *program* budgeting.

The critical characteristic common to both types of budgets is that the emphasis is shifted from the "input" of resources to the "output" of goods and services.

In the typical church budget items are listed as

objects: salaries, pension, auto allowance, building maintenance, fuel, electricity, telephone, mortgage payments, benevolence. If the list is complete and the figures are accurate, such a list will add up to the estimated expenditures for the coming year.

But such a listing says very little about what that church actually hopes to accomplish in the coming year other than to raise a certain number of dollars.

In performance and program budgets, the focus is not on the input of resources, but on output, on accomplishments and performance. A simple form of performance budget may be used by a person when he trades his car. Instead of saying, "It cost me $1,700 to trade," he explains to a friend, "I just traded cars and I figure it cost me 8.9 cents a mile to drive my old car for three years."

Or he may speak in program budget terms and say, "It cost me $1,150 to use my car in business, $200 for family needs, and $350 for recreation and travel."

A conventional church budget can be translated into either a performance or a program budget with some effort and creative thinking. For example, the group of items sometimes labeled "ministerial support," which includes the pastor's salary, pension, car allowance, and parsonage, can be made into a much more meaningful statement of performance such as this:

61 worship services @ $50	$3,050
117 hospital calls @ $3	351
197 church meetings @ $10	1,970
Instruction for 41 new members @ $30	1,230
387 home and business calls @ $2	774
300 hours pastoral counseling @ $5	1,500
600 hours administration @ $3	1,800

The nature of congregational life makes a performance budget of limited use except as a planning tool. In one parish, a performance budget similar to the above listing was prepared and distributed to all members. Later, the pastor called on a member in the hospital with a very mild illness. She responded to the call by saying, "Pastor, I'll be here for a few more days, but instead of calling on me again, just put the three dollars in the offering plate. I know the church needs the money."

A more useful budget results when attention is focused, not on the activities or performance of the pastor or the church staff, but rather on the entire congregation as one operation, or as a series of *programs*.

In such a program budget, the activities of the parish may be divided for purposes of analysis into three categories. The first is "congregational care" and refers to activities directed primarily to the members. This includes corporate worship, the church school, most of the cost of maintaining and operating the building, providing opportunities for the personal and spiritual growth of the members, the various organizations in the parish, pastoral care of members, and similar items.

The second category is "evangelism" and includes all efforts to reach and to assimilate into the life of the congregation the unchurched in the community. Here an estimate is made of the amount of the pastor's time and of the other resources of the church which are directed toward reaching the unchurched. A price tag is calculated for these efforts and is placed opposite evangelism in the program budget.

The third category carries the label "mission and witness" and basically includes two items. One is the amount of money contributed by the parish to the work of the church outside the parish, including denominational apportionments, gifts to church institutions such as hospitals, children's homes, colleges, seminaries, and similar expenditures.

The other is the allocation for witness and mission in the community. This might include gifts to the local council of churches, the net cost to the church of operating a day nursery, the expense involved in providing a meeting place for the local chapter of Alcoholics Anonymous, a portion of the pastor's support equivalent to the time he spends as a community leader, or the cost of the church's own neighborhood social welfare program.

It is relatively easy for someone familiar with the program of the parish to go through the local church budget and allocate the dollar amount for each budget category to one of these three categories. It is helpful to first prepare a performance budget, but that is not an essential step in the preparation of a program budget. In many cases, a single budget item may have to be apportioned among the three divisions. While the figures will not, and need not, be precise, they do provide a useful estimate of how the parish is dividing its financial resources.

In the actual process of preparing a program budget, most congregations use only a few broad general categories the first year, and then refine these and enlarge the number of categories in subsequent years as they gain experience in the process.

The preparation and use of such a simple form of program budget offers a half dozen benefits. First, it provides a simple and reasonably accurate index of the health of the parish. A church that finds it is allocating ninety percent of its dollar resources to

49

congregational care and only ten percent to evangelism and mission is sick, and very possibly on its deathbed. By contrast, the church that is spending forty or fifty or sixty percent of its dollars on evangelism and mission, both inside and outside the community, probably is in very good health.

A second value of this method of budget analysis is that it improves communication between the church and its members, helping them to understand what their church is doing and how their money is being spent. Very few members are aware of the many different ministries and activities carried on by their church. The program budget is a means of telling them.

Such a budget also provides a more creative analysis of parish expenditures than does the conventional budget. It gives the church council a meaningful framework for examining the issues involved in allocating resources. It provides both stimulus and one means of initiating a discussion about purpose and mission.

In one inner-city parish, for example, only ten percent of the total receipts are used for paying denominational apportionments and for other work outside the parish. By comparison with other churches, this looks bad. The average church in that denomination "sends away" an average of twenty-four percent of its total receipts to support the denominational program and to other "mission" endeavors.

A program budget, however, revealed that between fifty and sixty percent of this parish's total expenditures could be classified as either evangelism or witness and mission, and that only about forty to fifty percent is being allocated to congregational care.

Well over one half the pastor's time, for example, is spent in working with the unchurched families in the neighborhood around the church. A study of the use of the building revealed that three fourths of its use was directed to housing community programs and to specialized programs and ministries to non-members.

In this case, program budgeting helped the members of this inner-city church to gain a new understanding of themselves. Instead of being ashamed of their benevolence record, they saw themselves as a church "in mission" in the community. This process also helped denominational leaders and pastors of some larger churches to look beyond benevolence-giving in evaluating the performance of small inner-city parishes.

A fourth benefit lies in the reactions of the members. The program budget encourages reactions both from those who believe the church should concentrate on serving its members, and from those who believe greater emphasis should be placed on evangelism and mission. The dialogue induced by these reactions may produce some sparks, but it also can stimulate creative thinking about the definition of the purpose of the church in general and that parish in particular. It may be a useful means of encouraging the members to place greater emphasis on evangelism, outreach to the community and mission into the world.

A fifth, and to some people the most important value of the program budget is derived from its use in the "every-member canvass." Too often, teams of visitors go out with a copy of the conventional church budget and say, "Friends, we've come to solicit your pledge for next year. Our budget is up ten percent and we hope you will increase your pledge by ten percent." It is difficult to arouse people's enthusiasm in a discussion about the rising cost of property insurance, the increase in the postal rates, and the higher cost of utility services.

The program budget gives these visitors an outline for talking about money and costs in terms of the purposes of the church and the ministries and programs carried on by their parish. Instead of going out to talk about money, the visitors in the every-member canvass go out to talk about ministry and program. Instead of treating money as an end in itself, they place it in proper perspective as a means to an end. (A more detailed discussion of how this has been done in local churches can be found in the final section of this chapter.)

Finally, every congregation ought to attempt an answer to the question, "How much are we spending just to stay in existence as an institution, and how much are we spending on ministry?" One church decided to calculate how much of the total budget was spent on owning, maintaining, and operating the building. This was a fairly simple process, since it involved adding up such items as utilities, insurance, heat, janitorial services, and mortgage payments.

The budget committee was startled to discover that they were allocating 47 percent of their annual receipts to the building. Then they asked themselves, "Is that a lot or only average?" The direct answer is that it is a comparatively large percentage. Most Protestant congregations allocate between 15 and 35 percent of their receipts to the care and operation of their property.

By preparing a program budget, they were forced to ask basic questions about why they existed as a church. They were also given a way to find the answers.

PPBS

A possible next step in the process after adoption of the concept of a program budget is to make the budget preparation part of a larger process that includes planning, program development and implementation, and budgeting. In nearly every organization where this has been attempted in an effort to improve the quality of the budget preparation process and the usefulness of the budget, there has been some reluctance or opposition from individuals because this means a change from the traditional way of doing things. Therefore, it is reasonable to assume that any local church that begins to move in the direction of making the budget preparation a part of a more comprehensive planning process will encounter some resistance.

This concept of the budgeting process was developed in the mid-1950's and is called the *Planning–Programming–Budgeting System* or PPBS. It was used by Secretary Robert S. McNamara in the Department of Defense for several years, but did not gain widespread attention until after that day in August, 1965, when President Johnson ordered all federal departments to start using it. The Department of Health, Education, and Welfare was the second federal department to carry on extensive systematic research into use of PPBS, and it has been used with great effectiveness in the Department of Agriculture and the Office of Economic Opportunity.

Enough has now been learned about the concept, its advantages and its limitations, that it is attracting the attention of budget specialists, planners, and administrators in a variety of organizations and agencies. It is now being used in the Board of American Missions of the Lutheran Church in America and many other ecclesiastical organizations including scores of local churches.

What is its value? In general terms it offers seven possible benefits to the local church.

1. It provides a systematic framework for parish leaders which brings together planning, goal formulation, fiscal control, an analysis of the probable consequences of alternative courses of action, and projected costs into one understandable package. It helps the decision-makers see the whole picture.

2. It forces everyone involved to define objectives or goals more precisely.

3. It offers a systematic method of looking at alternative courses of action in terms of both costs and probable effectiveness. It helps to remind everyone that there is more than one answer to most parish problems.

4. It provides an objective basis *in advance* for evaluation of performance.

5. Inevitably, it will produce pressures which force parish leaders to think in terms of basic policies; and thus to develop policy guidelines rather than act by intuition on each matter as it comes up.

6. It clarifies what information and data are required and will be used in the decision-making process.

7. Perhaps most important of all, it places the emphasis on output or performance rather than on the input of money, buildings, manpower, and other resources.

The experiences of voluntary organizations that have adopted this planning–programming–budgeting approach have produced four caution signs that may be worth reading.

First, look around among the members for a person who has had some professional or academic experience with the concept. There are literally thousands of these laymen in parishes all across the nation. Utilize their skill and experience.

Second, be patient. Do not expect sudden miracles! Usually it takes at least three years from the day the system is inaugurated until major benefits become highly visible.

Third, the system will not solve problems. It simply enables the leadership to identify the problems more clearly and to open up new approaches to dealing with these problems.

Finally, it must be recognized that some people will be unhappy. In nearly every ecclesiastical organization the responsibility for the preparation of the budget has been separated from the responsibility for program development and implementation. If anyone has been doing any planning, this responsibility usually has been separated from either of these other two functions. When these three are combined into one process, it means a greater centralization of authority. It also frequently means that someone feels his empire has been invaded and he has lost some or all of his power. Few people respond to such a change with joy and enthusiasm!

Despite these caution signs, PPBS illustrates the tremendous possibilities inherent in a systematic approach to decision-making. It emphasizes the importance of looking at the budget in terms of output rather than input. It demonstrates that the budget preparation process can be turned from a chore into a vital tool for decision-makers. It also is one way to shift the emphasis from money to ministry in parish planning.

Ministry or Money?

Recently the chairman of the finance committee in a four-hundred-member Michigan parish was asked, "How are you planning to pledge your church's budget for the coming year?"

"We're not!" was his instantaneous response.

His reply startled the questioner. It also illustrated one of several responses that is gaining increasing popularity as parish leaders use the budget as the beginning point in an effort to plan more systematically for the work of that parish, and as they respond to the impact of inflation and rising costs. For discussion purposes, these responses can be grouped into three categories. The first delays the budget preparation process until *after* pledges have been received. The second emphasizes two-way communication. The third shifts the emphasis in the budget preparation process from precedent to purpose, program, and priorities.

Each one of these three methods represents a departure from traditional procedures. Each represents a response to a local problem which actually is widespread. Each relies on a degree of mutual trust that too often has been missing among members of the local church. Each one illustrates how local church leaders are trying to shift the emphasis in the budgeting process from dollars and pledges to people and program.

The first of these is illustrated by the layman's remark that in his church they did not plan to seek pledges to underwrite the coming year's budget. In previous years, members of the finance committee had prepared a tentative budget, enlisted a few helpers, and made a systematic effort to call at each home in the parish.

When the caller explained that he was seeking pledges for the church budget, he often was confronted with questions such as, "How much do you want from me?" or "How much do you need?" or "Why can't you get more people to help carry the load?"

In an attempt to break this pattern and to move from "pledging the budget" to a program of Christian stewardship, the leaders in this parish revised their procedures. With the approval of the church council, they decided to go out and ask members for pledges *before* preparing a budget. The callers had simple and clear responses to the questions which previously had been irksome if not diversionary. These responses were drawn from Paul's letters to the church at Corinth and a concept of stewardship based, not on what the church needs, but rather upon the idea of proportionate giving.

The second approach that has been gaining adherents is in part a response to such complaints as "The only time anyone from the church ever calls is when they want money," or "This parish is run by a small clique and they never listen to anyone but themselves," or "Why should I give when I don't have any voice in how the money is spent."

In this procedure, the every-member canvass for pledges, which usually is held in November, is preceded by an every-member visitation program. In some parishes there is one such effort in late April or early May and a second in late September or early October. In several congregations the spring visit is strictly a listening visit. The first fall visit is a "report back" visit in which the caller explained how the comments and suggestions gathered in the spring had been incorporated into the proposed program and asked for evaluative comments and for suggestions on the ordering of priorities. In others, this effort is limited to one round of visits prior to the every-member canvass.

Typically, a large corps of visitors is recruited— usually equal to ten to twenty percent of the confirmed membership. Usually the same person calls at the same households for both or all three of the calls that are made as a part of this process. These visitors meet together for a training program, usually two or three sessions, in which five "hows" are emphasized.

1. How to make a call.
2. How to listen (a very critical skill).
3. How to elicit fundamental complaints and suggestions from what may first appear to be superficial gripes.
4. How to respond to questions about the parish's purpose, goals, program, priorities, and limitations.
5. How to report what has been heard, so this data can be utilized in the decision-making process.

While the details of this program vary from parish to parish, the important feature is the establishment of meaningful two-way communication between the parish as an organization and the membership. A significant fringe benefit is that the training program produces a comparatively large corps of members who understand the purpose and goals of the parish, and are able to articulate these on various informal occasions through the year. In an attempt to maximize this fringe benefit, some parishes try to recruit a completely new corps of visitors each year.

In those congregations where the same person called at a member's home in the spring and again in the early autumn, it usually was relatively easy to keep the discussion focused on purpose, program, and priorities when this same person made a third call in the late fall for pledges.

A third procedural change that is gaining popularity has been motivated at least in part by the resistance to beginning with last year's budget. Too often the budget preparation process has meant that each member of the finance committee was given a copy of last year's budget and the process was simply one of going down the sheet and discussing whether each item should be reduced, increased, or held at the same figure.

As more and more laymen define the church in terms of mission and ministry rather than in terms of institutional maintenance, resistance to the old procedure increases and it becomes easier to use the budget preparation as the beginning point for a systematic approach to parish planning. Instead of beginning with precedent, the finance committee usually begins with one of these questions.

"What is our purpose?"

"What are the needs to which we should be responding?"

"What should be our priorities in allocating our resources?"

Each question puts the focus on ministry rather than on money. Each question places the emphasis on the end, or the goal, rather than on the means of achieving that goal. Each question makes the budget preparation a self-evaluation process. Each question strengthens the orientation toward today and tomorrow and away from yesterday.

In looking at these three approaches to the parish budget, it would be misleading, and irrelevant, to suggest these are new ideas that never have been tried before. What is important is that it appears a growing number of local church leaders are receptive to new or different approaches to budgeting parish finances.

In talking with pastors and laymen where these procedures have been followed, seven points stand out that may be of general interest.

1. The most important considerations in determining whether any of these procedures proved to be helpful can be summarized in three words—*communication, participation,* and *training.* Unless there was good internal two-way communication on what was being proposed and why, and unless there was widespread participation in planning and implementing the program, the results tended to fall short of expectations. Training was held to be an essential element in those parishes where the procedure followed or resembled either of the first two described here.

2. In most parishes, and in nearly all that used a procedure similar to the last two described here, there was widespread satisfaction with the shift in emphasis from dollars to purpose and program. As one layman said, after sharing in an every-member canvass that threw away the current budget and started with a blank slate, "For the first time since I've been a member here I hear people telling about the church as a religious organization rather than as a club that has to be kept alive. In the past the

THE EASIEST PLACE TO BEGIN

focus always was on money and survival rather than on program and ministry."

3. In those parishes where there was good internal communication, broad participation in the process, a major emphasis on purpose and goals, and adequate training for both those responsible for making decisions and those going out calling, the results ranged from gratifying to amazing. In an era when the leaders in many congregations were delighted to see a five percent increase in pledges, most of the parishes using one of these approaches, or some variation of them, were reporting pledges for the new budget running fifteen to one hundred percent above the previous year's total. Perhaps more important than the dollar increase represented by the pledges was the feeling symbolized in the comment of the layman who said, "In past years when we talked about pledging the budget there was a ceiling over the whole effort. Everyone could feel it. This year, when we talked about giving in response to how the Lord had blessed us, and about needs and about ministry, that ceiling disappeared."

In one parish, which devised a program that combined elements from all three of the procedures described here, fifty callers were trained to go out and call in 168 homes. These callers signed their own pledge cards for the new year before going out to call. These fifty pledges equaled ninety-seven percent of the total receipts for the previous year.

4. In those parishes that developed a visitation program that emphasized two-way communication and used a system of three calls, the most widespread reaction can be summed up in the comment of the woman who said, "Until I went out to call I never realized how little real awareness and how

61

much misinformation there exists about our church among the members."

5. Closely related has been the enthusiastic response of many parish leaders to the values in a systematic program that gave every member the opportunity to raise questions, articulate gripes and complaints, suggest a reordering of priorities, and offer proposals for a redefinition of purpose and program.

Even in those parishes where this was undertaken with limited enthusiasm and too few callers, the benefits usually exceeded expectations. When two-way communication is established, alienation is reduced, the "we-they" division is lessened, and the sense of community and common purpose is strengthened.

6. One of the most frequently offered comments is reflected in the admonition, "When you undertake a new approach such as we did, be sure to keep the members informed on what is happening!"

If the emphasis is on a visitation program, be sure to report what was heard by the visitors *and on how this has affected the program and ministry of the parish.*

If the emphasis is on a redefinition of purpose, share the new statement of purpose *and the implications of this statement with all of the members.*

If the emphasis is on a reconsideration of priorities, report on what was decided and why.

If the emphasis is on mission and ministry rather than on money, report to the entire parish how the members responded.

The more channels of communication that are opened and used in the parish, and the more two-way communication that flows through those channels, the healthier the parish.

7. Finally, if in your parish you are discontented with the current approach to parish finances, if you believe that your parish has a worse case of institutional blight than any other congregation in the world, and if you have concluded that these suggestions will solve all of the problems in your parish, please sleep on it for one more night! One of the problems of any voluntary association that must be financially self-supporting is the tendency to put survival above all other goals. The budget preparation process and the every-member canvass offer opportunities for beginning a parish planning process that shifts the emphasis back to purpose and performance, but just as there usually is more than one answer to any problem, there is no one answer that will solve all problems. You may want to look for additional ideas as you deal with the issues of blight and renewal in your parish.

SUGGESTIONS FOR FURTHER READING

"Social Goals and Indicators for American Society." *The Annals of the American Academy of Political and Social Science*, May 1967 and September 1967.

Bauer, Raymond A., ed. *Social Indicators*. Cambridge, Mass.: M.I.T. Press, 1966.

Botner, Stanley B. "Four Years of PPBS: An Appraisal." *Public Administration Review*, July/ August 1970.

Hartley, Harry J. *Educational Planning–Programming–Budgeting*. Englewood Cliffs, N. J.: Prentice-Hall, 1968.

Hinrichs, Harley H. and Taylor, Graeme M., eds. *Program Budgeting and Benefit–Cost Analysis*. Pacific

3
BLIGHT, SELF-RENEWAL, AND INNOVATION

"Some men who boast of having had twenty years of experience actually have had only one year of experience, they simply have repeated that one year twenty times," commented the personnel officer for a large corporation. The discussion concerned the value of experience versus education in evaluating candidates for managerial positions. He was contending that some men settle into a narrow rut very early in life while others continue to grow, and that simply counting the number of years of experience may not be very helpful in evaluating prospective employees.

In his provocative book, *Self-Renewal*, John Gardner suggests that in some parts of our society a combination of apathy, rigidity, and moral emptiness is producing a condition he refers to as dry rot, a condition, incidentally that is significantly different from decay. Gardner argues that the only hope for countering this natural tendency leading to societal dry rot is to produce men and women with the capacity for self-renewal. He contends that in every social enterprise, aging, lowered motivation, routine repetition, suppression of the individual, declining vitality, apathy, and rigid specialization tend to go together and to lead to the decline of that organization or society.

Both of these men are referring to a condition that may be described with one word—blight. A dictionary definition of blight suggests that it is a condition in which there is a withering and a cessation of growth that frustrates plans and hope.

Both individuals and organizations are vulnerable to the ravages of blight. It can be seen in the teacher who has not read a new book in ten yers, in the preacher who goes to the barrel for nearly every sermon after his first or second pastorate, in the housewife who is following exactly the same daily routine that she followed twenty years ago, in the secretary who, as she moves from job to job, sees absolutely no differences between her work and responsibilities in her present position and the last place she was employed, in the doctor who is prescribing the same drugs today that he prescribed back in 1955, and in the salesman who fails to recognize the changing needs of his clientele.

Social organizations also are subject to blight. Those that are immune to the economic competition of the market place tend to have the higher degree of vulnerability. The local church is as vulnerable to blight as any other voluntary association, and this condition probably is the largest single obstacle in the parish planning process.

Forms of Institutional Blight in the Parish

It may be helpful in responding to this ever present challenge of blight to identify a half dozen of the forms of institutional blight that frequently are found in the local church. This listing is not intended to be exhaustive or to establish mutually exclusive categories. The intent is primarily one of identifying and illustrating the nature of the problem.

One of the most common is the desire to achieve those circumstances that will increase the institutional security of the local church. The symptoms of this condition often are revealed in such phrases as these. "It will be wonderful when we can have our own full-time pastor." "In another six months we should be financially self-supporting." "We are planning a special drive to build the endowment fund up to at least one million dollars." "We'll be in good shape here if we can get our membership total back above the five-hundred level." "The first priority is to re- place this old structure with a new modern build- ing." "In another five years this will be the largest Protestant congregation in the county."

Closely related to this, but much less subtle, is the blight that accompanies the drive for institutional survival. Unlike the condition described above where the basic institutional focus is on security, in these congregations the emphasis is simply on survival. "If this church doesn't begin to get some new members it will die." "If we can't reach the youth, there won't be any church in a few years." "We have to take in at least five new families next year or we won't be able to pay our bills." Statements such as these indicate the survival of the institution is clearly at stake. Survival goals have come to dominate the decision-making process and have completely smothered any sense of ministry or mission. People are viewed as objects to be manipulated and exploited on behalf of the institu- tion, rather than as children of God, each with his own distinctive needs.

A third form of blight, and one that can be found in nearly every organization, is the tendency to ignore future consequences of current actions. Today the importance of considering the consequences is receiving a much-needed emphasis by the new concern for ecology. During the past few years the media have been filled with horror stories about the consequences of man's failure to consider the environmental and ecological results of his actions. The blight of pollution is one result of this failure to consider the future consequences of current actions.

The parallels in the local church are many. One is the congregation that goes into a building program that taxes its financial capability for a dozen years into the future. When the new building is completed, it is discovered there is no program money available for use of the new structure. Another is the parish that uses the "convenience schedule" on Sunday morning which places worship and church school in the same hour. A decade later people wonder "Why are none of those children who were in Sunday school a few years ago attending worship now?" A third is the local church where the basic purpose of the men's club or the women's organization gradually has been changed from service to fellowship. A few years later the older members cannot understand why the young men and the young women are not interested in their organization.

Another form of institutional blight that is widespread is the tendency to plan for yesterday. This is illustrated by the aging congregation that has dispersed and now most of the active members live five or ten miles from the meeting place. Today, for the first time, they believe they have the financial capability to build the church school they needed fifteen years ago when this really was a neighborhood church with many young couples in the membership.

Another expression of this same form of blight is to use the wants and needs of the leaders as a representative model of the entire congregation. This is illustrated by the common tendency to plan on the assumption that any program or schedule that fulfills the needs and satisfies the wants of those doing the planning also will meet the wants and needs of everyone else. This was, and is, a common assumption in many congregations, but it certainly is a fallacious assumption in planning for today and tomorrow!

A fifth form of institutional blight is the tendency in every organization to turn the means of fulfilling a basic purpose of the organization into an end in itself.

In hundreds of congregations the original reasons for establishing the Sunday school have been forgotten and the maintenance of the Sunday school has become an end in itself, often at the expense of the educational function of the parish. Similarly, great sacrifices are made to finance the construction of an obviously needed new building, but the policies determining the use of that building are influenced more by maintenance considerations than by a desire to respond to people's needs. Likewise, for many church members *attendance* at corporate worship has replaced the concept of *participation* in worship.

Perhaps the most subtle form of institutional blight in any organization can be found in the reporting. Whether it is an annual report for the organization, a report on the results of a special project, or the report of the work of a subcommittee, the basic tendency is to emphasize (a) activities (number of meetings, miles traveled, attendance and other "inputs"), or (b) that which is most easily counted or measured, or (c) that which sounds most interesting, or (d) that which will enhance the apparent importance of the person doing the reporting. The tendency to place the emphasis on these aspects of the subject often mean there is no comparison of performance with purpose or of results with expectations. Thus, the reporting process, instead of clarifying purpose, goals, expectations, alternatives, and results, frequently obscures these with a mass of trivial, irrelevant, or diversionary data.

These illustrations of the forms and expressions of institutional blight emphasize the importance of this problem and the need to be aware of it in the parish planning process. It is unrealistic to expect to completely eliminate institutional blight in any organization managed by sinful human beings, but recognizing the existence of the problem is the first step in reducing it to controllable proportions.

There are several useful approaches to reducing the severity of institutional blight. They overlap and are mutually interdependent, but can be discussed most clearly by separating them. The first is to replace the functional blindness which encourages blight in an organization with a capability for self-renewal. A second is for members to become more skillful in introducing new ideas into the organization. The third is to strengthen the lines of accountability and to build in a process of continuing self-evaluation.

The Self-Renewing Congregation

The life cycle of most organizations tends to be a pattern of growth followed by a leveling off period and a challenge or opportunity for renewed growth.

Sometimes this challenge is accepted and a period of new growth occurs followed by another period of leveling off. Up to this point the pattern resembles a rising staircase. Eventually, however, in most organizations the challenge to move on to a new step produces a major crisis. Sometimes the adverse factors in this crisis are overcome and the stairstep progression upward is resumed. In other cases, however, the crisis proves to be overwhelming and is followed by disintegration, demoralization, and the death of the organization.

This pattern also describes the life cycle of literally thousands of Protestant congregations that have disappeared from the religious scene in the United States. Some succumbed at the first crisis. Others overcame the first or second and sometimes even the third and fourth crises, but eventually they also succumbed.

From this somewhat oversimplified description, the question arises, "How can a local congregation be prepared to overcome the crisis?"

Forty years ago, after studying hundreds of urban churches, the pioneer church planner of American Protestantism, H. Paul Douglass, declared that any urban congregation that did not develop the ability to adapt to changing conditions was doomed to extinction. The passage of time has supported the validity of that statement, but what is it that enables a congregation to adapt to changing circumstances?

In 1965, John Gardner published an article, "How to Prevent Organizational Dry Rot," that suggested nine rules for organizational renewal. This approach is more helpful than the simple admonition to adapt. It is possible to look at the congregations that have been able to adapt to changing conditions and to see several characteristics that enabled them to be in fact self-renewing organizations. Three of these parallel three of Gardner's rules for the prevention of organizational dry rot.

1. The self-renewing congregation operates from a balanced definition of purpose. The outsider looking at these congregations frequently sees three highly visible emphases in their life and program: (a) an effective effort to help people find meaning in life, and especially to cope with the fundamental issues of life, (b) a recognition of the need and place of celebration in the life of the individual and of the congregation, and (c) an operational definition of the call to servanthood.

Or, to put it another way and to pick up the thread that runs through chapter 6, the members of the self-renewing congregation know who they are and where they are going.

2. The self-renewing congregation is able to distinguish between the message it has to deliver and the method that is appropriate at that time and place for delivering the message. Two of the most highly visible examples of congregations that have been able to make this distinction are (a) the congregation that once served a narrowly and clearly defined nationality, language, or social class constituency and now is ministering to a different constituency, and (b) the congregation that today is able to establish and carry on an effective and meaningful ministry to the 16–24 age group and also to the 30–60 age group.

3. The self-renewing congregation is able to reach, receive, accept, and assimilate newcomers into the life of the fellowship and the life of celebration and servanthood. (This parallels the second and third

rules of John Gardner's for preventing dry rot in an organization.) This almost never happens in a congregation with more than 60 to 75 members unless there is a deliberate, conscious, and intentional effort to make it happen.

4. The self-renewing congregation is more sensitive to the contemporary needs of people and to the necessity of responding to those needs than it is to continuing customs, maintaining traditions, and preserving old structures of organization. These congregations also recognize that the needs of people vary among individuals and from time to time. The needs of the reader of this paragraph will not be the same day after day for the next decade.

5. The members of the self-renewing congregation not only know what their church is doing, they believe in what their parish is doing. They believe the life and ministry of their church is important to themselves and to others. This belief is communicated to the outsider.

6. The self-renewing congregation recognizes that from time to time it will encounter a threatening or disruptive crisis, but the members expect to overcome that crisis.

7. The self-renewing congregation has a redundant and effective system of internal communication. There are no secrets and few disruptive surprises in such a parish.

8. The self-renewing congregation has a built-in provision for self-criticism (Gardner's third rule). It encourages the expression of differences of opinion and the criticism of leaders by one another and by non-leaders which enables this to lead to creative and constructive dialogue. It does not, however, make this a game or an end in itself. "The creative use of

conflict" has become a popular phrase in church circles and increasingly appears to be identified as an end rather than as a means. This is a burden the self-renewing congregation does not have to bear.

9. The self-renewing congregation is not overly dependent on one leader such as the pastor or "the key layman." Leadership is required and it is present, but it is shared, not monopolized. Furthermore, the best leadership is concerned with ministry and service rather than with institutional maintenance.

10. The self-renewing congregation sees itself as *one* of the institutional expressions of Christ's church. It does not identify itself as *the* church or as God's last hope for the salvation of mankind. No one congregation filled with mortal men can overcome a major crisis while carrying that burden.

Sooner or later the reader may raise a question about this list and the comments in the section "What Makes a Difference?" near the end of chapter 5. Obviously, there is considerable overlap. There is, however, a very basic important distinction. This list of some of the characteristics of the self-renewing congregation is based on studies of local churches that have been confronted with a crisis that could have caused the decline and demise of that congregation. Instead of dying, however, these local churches overcame the crisis and moved on into a new era of effective ministry. The checklist in chapter 5 is drawn from congregations that were able to develop a plan of action and to implement that plan. There is a difference.

"The greatest invention of the nineteenth century was the invention of the method of invention," declared Alfred North Whitehead in a book published in 1926. The reference is to the fact that during the nineteenth century men began on a large scale to deliberately set out to devise new ways of solving problems and meeting needs. As they did, they developed a systematic or "scientific method" of producing new inventions.

The companion to this in the twentieth century has been the development of a theory of how new ideas can be introduced into an organization. The value of such a theory and its relevance to this subject of institutional blight quickly becomes apparent when three basic propositions are lifted up for scrutiny. First, a fundamental cause of institutional blight is the failure to adapt to changing conditions. Second, the critical factor in any organization's ability to adapt to changing conditions is its capacity to accept and act upon new ideas. Third, as James Q. Wilson has suggested, the very factors that tend to encourage the presentation of new ideas also tend to be the factors that cause the organization to reject innovation.

Perhaps the most helpful way to suggest how these insights can be applied in the local church is to translate what has been learned from the study of organizational behavior into the context of the parish.

Innovation in the Parish

"Well, how did it go? What was their response to your plan?" With these words Mrs. Rogers greeted her husband as he came home late one evening after a long meeting at St. Paul's Church.

"Not one of those idiots could recognize a good idea if it hit him in the middle of the face! You never saw so much cold water dumped on any proposal so quickly as happened tonight. It's meetings like this one that make me wonder how the pastor can preach about love and understanding on Sunday, and in the same church only two days later, there can be so much suspicion, distrust, and negative thinking," raged her husband, who was obviously both bitter and disillusioned.

"What are you going to do now?" inquired his wife.

"I don't know, but I know what I'm *not* going to do," he barked. "I'm resigning from the church council and I am never going to serve on another committee or board in this parish. I'm through!"

One evening that same week Mrs. White greeted her husband as he came home from a meeting at Trinity Church. "Well, how did it go? What was their response to your bright idea?"

"It was a perfectly normal, predictable reaction," ruefully responded Mr. White. "Everyone present was absolutely opposed to what I suggested."

"What will you do next?" inquired his wife.

"Well, I'll have to think about this some more," was the response. "I should have known better than to come in cold with what I guess must have struck some of the folks as a pretty radical proposal, although it seemed to me to have such obvious merit, I thought at least some of the people would see the advantages. I guess I'll have to give more thought to my strategy."

Both Mr. Rogers and Mr. White are innovative individuals. Each was attempting to introduce a new idea for a new ministry into the ongoing life and program of his local church. Each was completely convinced of the merits and validity of his proposal. Each encountered complete and total rejection when he tried to gain support for his idea for change.

The big difference between the two was that Mr.

Rogers quickly became disillusioned with his fellow church members because of their failure to grasp the value of his new idea. By contrast, Mr. White realized the negative reaction he encountered was the normal response to a new idea. While he made a mistake in strategy, he recognized the mistake was his and did not blame his fellow members for his own error. Mr. White realized that if he wanted to receive approval for his new idea he would have to give more thought to how it was presented, and to the process of securing approval for innovative proposals.

Before examining the process of innovation, it may be helpful to review the three major sources of innovation in any organization or social system.

One of the major sources of innovation in our society is a crisis. If the church building burns to the ground tonight, a variety of interesting new ideas about solving this problem of a meeting place for the congregation will be offered by tomorrow noon. If the defense plant just outside town closes and one third of the families in the church move away, the resulting crisis in the parish is almost certain to produce some new ideas about parish programming and finances. The current crisis in which the Sunday school finds itself is producing several very significant innovations in the whole field of Christian education.

When thousands of Americans lost their life savings in the bank failures of the Great Depression, this crisis produced the Federal Deposit Insurance Corporation (FDIC), an innovation that provides for insuring bank deposits. The crisis of World War II produced the atom bomb, a major innovation in warfare. The wage freeze during the second world war led to an innovation in compensation with tremendous long-term social significance. This was the funded pension system for hourly workers. The housing shortage of the late 1960's produced an innovation in the role of the federal government in the housing industry. In addition to subsidizing construction, as had been the practice for over thirty years, a subsidy for occupancy was added in the Housing Act of 1968. The current crisis in environmental pollution is certain to produce several new ideas for dealing with this issue.

The second major source of innovation is "the outsider." This is the person who comes into an organization from the outside and brings new ideas from this "outside" perspective.

In the local church the traditional source of innovation from the "outside" has been either the new pastor, who brought ideas with him as he came to a new parish, or the denomination which developed new ideas for program and ministry and sought to introduce these into the life of the local church. In recent years, however, there has been increasing resistance to ideas and programs generated at the denominational headquarters and "handed down" to the people in the parish. It is worth noting that to a very remarkable degree this resistance has been encouraged by denominational leaders who have vigorously supported the concept that ideas for program and ministry should originate in the parish.

Couple with this trend the gradual change in the role of the pastor from that of the leader or doer or innovator to that of an enabler or coach or teacher and it might be concluded that innovation via "the outsider" is on the decline. This is not the case, however, for a new innovator from the outside is appearing with increasing frequency in the local church. This is the member who recently moved into the community and has transferred his church membership. This new member brings with him the remembrance of a set of experiences in previous parishes. Not infrequently, these become the basis for new ideas that he suggests might be tried in this parish.

One of the major assets of the outsider as an innovator is that frequently he "doesn't know any better." He has not yet been conditioned to the limitations of the situation that others accept without question. Local customs, precedents, and traditions have not yet handcuffed him.

A third, and often a more fruitful source of new ideas than either the outsider or a crisis, is what can be described as "the vision and model" concept.

The most widely known use of the vision and model concept has been the county agricultural agent. In 1937, the youthful, but wise, county agent in Iowa, who had graduated from the agricultural college of the state university only a few years earlier, did not drop in on a fifty-five-year-old farmer and announce, "I'm here to tell you how you can be a better farmer." Instead he sought out a respected farmer in that part of the county and suggested that next year he might want to divide that long field parallel to the road into three sections. In the first section he could plant the conventional seed after spreading barn manure over the field. In the middle section he might want to try the new hybrid seed corn with conventional fertilizer, and in the third section he could use the same hybrid seed with a new fertilizer. In August, farmers from all over the county were invited to come over and compare the three sections. They came, they saw a vision of what could be done, and they went home with a working model of how to do it.

79

Today an adaptation of the same concept to local church administration is illustrated by the layman who goes off to a conference or a workshop or on a field trip and comes back greatly excited over what he saw and heard, and is eager to put these new ideas into practice in his home church. In the best of these experiences he has "seen a vision" of what could happen and also studied a model of *how* this vision has been implemented elsewhere.

This is one of the major reasons for the great variety of church-sponsored workshops and seminars, field trips, retreats, and training programs that are held every year. In many of these a variety of opportunities are offered for participants to see a vision, study a real life situation in which that idea has been turned into practice, and ask questions as they consider how this could be adapted to their situation "back home."

Sometimes the "vision and model" comes from an item in the newspaper, an article in a church magazine, a book, or a chance conversation with a member of another parish. The greater the degree of personal involvement and the richer the opportunities for reflection, the more fruitful is the use of the vision and model concept of introducing new ideas into an organization.

These three sources tend to produce new ideas at a faster pace each year. The sources are growing more rapidly than is the capacity to absorb new ideas and to adjust to change. This leads back to the problem of Mr. Rogers and Mr. White. When you have a good idea, how do you get people to listen? How do you move from the source of new ideas to their implementation?

Innovation is not the only road to planned social change and it is not always a smooth road. The change-oriented individual who chooses this route should be aware of the conditions that may facilitate or impede innovation. One of the first things he should investigate is the environment for innovation. The environment is affected by the person interested in change and by the organization.

The most important element, and perhaps the critical factor in this environment, is the individual's view of other people. If he assumes they have closed minds, if he assumes that change comes only through conflict, if he assumes people are firmly wedded to the status quo, he might as well write off innovation as a source of change.

On the other hand, if he sincerely does believe that people do have within themselves the potential for growth, for change, and for adaptation, he may be more likely to find innovation an attractive alternative to reform or revolution.

A second critical element in a favorable environment for innovation is an orientation toward the needs of people rather than toward the maintenance of the institution. This is of fundamental importance in both social innovation and technological innovation! The agricultural county agent in the middle third of this century, who was attempting to strengthen and enlarge his organizational empire, was far less successful as a change agent than his counterpart in another county who went out and listened to the farmers, sought to identify their needs and to encourage them to try new methods of farming.

Theodore Levitt in his book *Innovation in Marketing* has pointed out that the company that concentrates on selling its own product often goes out of business while the company that places the primary emphasis on meeting the needs of its clientele opens the door wide for innovation.

A parallel can be drawn with the local church that concentrates on reversing the tide of a declining Sunday school attendance rather than on developing a Christian education program to meet contemporary needs.

A parallel can be drawn with the community organization that increasingly concentrates its resources on building up its membership rather than on responding to the needs of people in the neighborhood.

A third requirement for a favorable environment is the four T's—trust, time, talk, and tolerance.

The social innovator rarely can be effective unless people *trust* him. Unless this base of trust exists, the chances of failure are very great.

The effective social innovator is willing—although sometimes reluctantly so—to spend *time* discussing new ideas with others, to *talk* with both supporters and opponents, to take the time necessary to build a supporting group and to wait while others try to grasp the vision he has seen or recognize the crisis he perceived much earlier. The wise man knows that sometimes he must put off until tomorrow what can be put off until tomorrow. Or, to use the terminology of a wise old Indiana pastor, "Don't whip the horse until you have your feet in the stirrups."

Everyone involved in the change process should quickly recognize the need for *toleration* of diverse points of view. An intolerance of diversity is one of the most effective means of thwarting change. An openness to, and genuine tolerance of, differing ideas and diverse proposals for action is one of the means of facilitating change through innovation.

A fourth condition that affects the environment for innovation is the attitude of members of the organization toward people who ask questions. A willingness to depart from routine, a recognition of the potential contributions of creative persons, and an appreciation of the naturally curious individual with an unusually inquisitive mind are characteristics of the organization that offers a hospitable environment for innovation. These characteristics can be enhanced through intentionality.

In addition to a hospitable environment for innovation, the person who seeks to introduce new ideas into an organization would be well advised to keep several other factors in mind as he plans his strategy. The first of these was mentioned earlier, but it is difficult to overemphasize the point. In the parish, as in every other organization and social system, the normal reaction to innovation is rejection. Mr. Rogers did not understand this and mistakenly blamed his fellow members for being shortsighted in not eagerly accepting his proposal. Mr. White knew this, but in his enthusiasm over his own proposal he temporarily forgot it. Victor A. Thompson has noted that the creative process tends to be characterized by a refusal to make quick favorable judgments, a refusal to grasp an opportunity when it first appears, and a tendency to withhold commitment to a new idea. It would have saved some wear and tear on Mr. Rogers' temper if he had been aware of this.

The biggest single obstacle in the path of the would-be-innovator in the parish is that he frequently fails to remember that church members are people and, except in time of crisis, they tend to behave like normal human beings. This means they will naturally reject any new idea, *especially if it means a departure from the status quo!*

The innovator who does not recognize this response as normal and natural often becomes disillusioned and may even become bitter about what he believes is a rejection of him as a person rather than what is usually only a normal, negative, institutional response to a new idea.

The initial, almost automatic, rejection of a new idea is most often found among (a) the officially chosen leaders of the organization, (b) persons in the 25–50 age range, and (c) persons who once had a close personal attachment to the organization but now are not actively involved in or related to it, but who continue to have sentimental ties to it. (In this generalization such words and phrases as parish, armed services, university, corporation, seminary, governmental agency, or community association could be substituted for the word organization.)

It should also be remembered that the vast majority of changes of all types, whether they be innovations or reforms, that eventually are accepted and implemented are initially rejected. The local church that decided to relocate rather than to construct an addition to the old building frequently first rejected the proposal to relocate, went ahead with plans to build or remodel, and then reversed that with a decision to relocate. The union of two congregations to produce a new parish frequently was first rejected by one of the parties before the merger proposal was reactivated and adopted. The proposal to change to two worship services on Sunday morning often is rejected once or twice before it is later adopted.

The knowledgeable innovator recognizes this as part of the process and thus is neither disillusioned nor defeated by an initial rejection of a new idea. While this repeated emphasis on the normal tendency to reject every new idea the first time it is presented may sound very discouraging to some, this should not be the interpretation placed on this tendency. It should be remembered that the vast majority of all new ideas turn out to be poor ideas and should be rejected! This initial rejection may be a natural screening process that operates on the assumption a good idea cannot be killed with one blow.

A second important factor in the process of change by innovation centers on the recruitment of a group of allies who will help secure adoption of the new idea. As he seeks allies in his effort to win approval of his new idea, the effective innovator may find it helpful to incorporate some of these suggestions into his strategy.

1. Frequently it is wiser to rely more on the informal channels of communication than on the formal channels. The formal channels tend to be tied to the preservation of the status quo and, therefore, the innovator often must depend on informal channels to get his message through to potential supporters.

2. It always is helpful to be open and receptive to suggestions for refinement and improvement of the proposal. It is highly probable that others may have some wisdom to contribute on the subject! Furthermore, the people who

feel they have had a meaningful part in developing a new idea tend to be the ones who are most enthusiastic in supporting and implementing it.

3. *Unlike other forms of planned change,* innovation is basically the adding of something new, rather than the reform or replacement of an existing element of the program. The effective innovator, therefore, emphasizes that what he is proposing is change by addition, not change by alteration, or change by subtraction.

For example, if he is interested in contemporary forms of worship, he will *not* suggest a drastic alteration of the traditional Sunday morning worship service. Instead he will suggest that, perhaps *in addition* to this traditional service, the parish might be able to minister to more people by adding a contemporary worship service to the schedule, perhaps on Sunday evening, perhaps early Sunday morning, perhaps on another day of the week.

4. Among the allies who join the cause there should be some who have resources that will help in this process of securing approval and in the implementation of the innovative proposal. These resources take many forms— specialized skills, time, money, enthusiasm, prestige, influence, persistence, friends, and an openness to the new and different.

5. Most people respond more readily and more enthusiastically to that which is emotionally valuable to the group or organization. In other words, rational arguments may sound impressive, but occasionally they are not overwhelmingly persuasive!

6. The person who accepts the leadership responsibility for introducing a new idea into an organization must be able and willing to *vigorously* support and promote his innovative proposal! In any form of planned change persistence is important, but nowhere is a vigorous and persistent approach more important than in innovation. Among other things this means the innovator tends to be more visible than the reformer who is attempting to secure change by alteration or subtraction rather than by addition.

Finally, there is a third factor that is of tremendous long-term influence in both the organization's capability to provide a hospitable environment for innovation and the individual's ability to make effective use of that hospitable environment. This is the innovator's response to the final decision to adopt or reject his proposal and to the subsequent evaluation of that decision. The effective innovator is the person who is willing to share the credit generously for successes, and to carry gracefully by himself the blame for the failures. Since most people find it more comfortable to function in a reverse manner, and since most new ideas fail, this is a very large demand!

This also may be one reason why some people prefer change through revolution rather than by innovation. In a revolution any failure is always someone else's fault!

The other approach to the problem of blight that was mentioned earlier is based on the two words evaluation and accountability. It is impossible to talk about evaluation and accountability, however, without also introducing such issues as purpose,

87

quality, and the measurements of performance. That deserves a chapter by itself.

SUGGESTIONS FOR FURTHER READING

Bennis, Warren G., ed. *American Bureaucracy.* Chicago: Aldine Publishing Co., 1970.

————. *Organization Development: Its Nature, Origins and Prospects.* Reading, Mass.: Addison-Wesley Publishing Co., 1969.

Douglass, H. Paul. *The Church in the Changing City.* New York: George H. Doran, 1927.

Drucker, Peter F. *Landmarks of Tomorrow.* New York: Harper & Row, 1959.

Fisher, Wallace E. *Preface to Parish Renewal.* Nashville: Abingdon Press, 1968.

Gardner, John W. "How to Prevent Organizational Dry Rot." *Harpers Magazine,* October 1965.

————. *Self-Renewal.* New York: Harper & Row, 1963.

Kloetzli, Walter. *The City Church: Death or Renewal.* Philadelphia: Muhlenberg Press, 1961.

Levitt, Theodore. *Innovation in Marketing.* New York: McGraw-Hill, 1962.

Schon, Donald A. *Technology and Change.* New York: Delacorte Press, 1967.

Thompson, Victor A. *Bureaucracy and Innovation.* Tuscaloosa: University of Alabama Press, 1969.

Whitehead, Alfred N. *Science and the Modern World.* New York: The Macmillan Co., 1926.

Wilson, James A. "Innovation in Organization: Notes Toward a Theory" in James D. Thompson, ed. *Approaches to Organizational Design.* Pittsburgh: The University of Pittsburgh Press, 1966.

4

PURPOSE, EXPECTATIONS, AND EVALUATION

"We keep hearing that the church tends to react to trends and conditions in the world around us. Whether we like it or not, that does seem to be the case. As I understand the story, the first studies by churchmen in church and community were a response to the migration from rural America to the cities back in the first two or three decades of this century," commented a young minister at a pastor's school.

"For fifteen or twenty years after the close of World War II one of the dominant trends in the United States was the movement out of the central cities to the suburbs. The response of the churches was a big wave of new church development," he continued. "In the 1950's we began to hear a lot about the inner city and the churches responded by taking a new look at the role and the future of congregations in the inner city. This was followed by the churches' involvement in the struggle for racial justice and the big emphasis in the mid-60's on community organization. Along about the same time the churches joined President Lyndon B. Johnson's unconditional war on poverty and then in 1970 the question of ecology was added to the list and in many parts of the church it became the top item on the agenda."

"Now what I want to know," he concluded, "is what single trend or movement in this country is going to have the greatest impact on the churches, and especially on the parish, in the next ten years?"

This young pastor was asking a very difficult, but a very important question. It would be easier to list twenty trends than to identify the one that will have the greatest impact. It is possible, however, to name one trend that will have a rapidly growing impact on the planning process in tens of thousands of local churches.

This is the quest for quality.

Until recently the primary emphasis in the United States has been on quantity rather than quality, on activity rather than performance, and on efficiency rather than effectiveness. The old pattern can be seen in the churches where the number of members and the attendance at Sunday school have been two of the most commonly used criteria for evaluation. The old pattern is illustrated by the economic indicators that have measured the gross national product rather than either the quality of that product or the cost to the nation in producing those goods and services. The old pattern also is illustrated by the twin yardsticks of efficiency and economy that have constituted the traditional basis for evaluating governmental operations.

The new pattern can be seen in the weather forecasts that now include three or four indicators describing the quality of the air, and amount of carbon monoxide, sulphur dioxide, dust, and dirt in the air. This new emphasis on quality is illustrated by the growing concern about the quality of life in the city. This same emphasis on quality is behind the demand that the government develop a system of social reporting that would provide relevant data on the quality of life in the United States. This new emphasis also can be seen in the rapid growth during the past few years of the consumer movement. For example, it required thirty years for the monthly *Consumer Reports*, founded back in 1936, to reach the million mark in circulation. In the next four years, the circulation nearly doubled.

For those concerned with the life of the local church, perhaps the most relevant illustration of this growing emphasis on quality is the public school system. For decades the public schools were being evaluated on the basis of such criteria as average daily attendance, the proportion of the faculty with a bachelor's or master's degree, the teacher-pupil ratio, the average annual expenditures per pupil, the age of the buildings, the proportion of entering students who dropped out before graduation, and the percentage of high school graduates going on to college. Most of these criteria represented attempts to measure quantity, activity, or economy rather than quality.

Today a new emphasis is being placed on quality. Parents are not content to know the teacher-pupil ratio; they want to know what is happening to the children in that classroom. There is a growing recognition by the general public that the number of children failing a grade can be reduced without improving the educational quality of the school. It has been demonstrated that expenditures per pupil can be increased and the dropout rate can be cut without changing the quality of the educational program.

One example of the result of this new emphasis on quality can be found in Gary, Indiana. There a private company has been engaged to take complete charge of the Banneker Elementary School. This company will be paid $800 per pupil, but it must refund this fee for each student that is below the national achievement norm after three years in school. Instead of a payment based on the cost of services or on enrollment, the payment is geared to quality. There are now more than a score of similar contracts between local school districts and private educational firms in various parts of the nation.

What would be the response in a parish if a group of parents said, "The size of our pledge for next year will be proportional to what happens to our children who are attending the church school"?

While the issue of performance may not be raised in many congregations in these exact terms, it appears certain that more questions are going to be asked about quality in an increasing number of local churches in the years to come.

As local churches are forced to deal with this issue of quality and performance, the discussion naturally turns to the subject of evaluation, and especially to the need for self-evaluation. Before turning to that subject, however, it may be helpful to review some of the characteristics of the local church that affect the planning process in the parish.

Characteristics of the Local Church

In planning for the mission and ministry of the local church it may be helpful to keep in mind three characteristics of the local church that occasionally are overlooked. Each of the three is very important in planning for the future of the parish.

The first is that in many respects the local church is a social organization or institution that tends to function in a manner similar to other institutions in our society. Therefore, much can be learned that will be helpful in parish planning by studying the organizational behavior of other institutions.

The second is that the local church must always be viewed by its members, not simply as another of many organizations in the community, but as a part of the universal church established by Jesus Christ. In discussing the purpose of the local church, the members do not begin with a blank slate. They begin with a set of "givens" that are found in the New Testament. The local church is not an institution in which the members decide what they want it to be and then set out to achieve those goals.

A Christian church, by definition, has a unique place in that all the members have joined in a common covenant in which they acknowledge Jesus Christ as lord and savior. This places certain unique limitations on the definition of purpose, on the formulation of goals, and on the program of that institution known as the local church. It also places certain unique obligations on that organization and on its members. These obligations and limitations must be recognized as the members define the response of that specific congregation to the call of the Lord, as they prepare a definition of the purpose of that congregation in that community at this point in human history, as they formulate goals and objectives for that parish, and as they move on to implement that purpose in the development of a program of ministry and service.

The third characteristic of the local church that tends to be neglected is its resiliency. The church is tough. The worshiping congregation and the family are the only two social institutions that have persisted in much the same form for nineteen centuries. That is a point that should be kept in mind when encountering those predictions that contend the local church is obsolete and will soon disappear and the family will no longer exist as a social unit in the year 2000.

All three of these points are of crucial importance in the process of self-evaluation by which the members periodically examine the organization, operation, and work of their local church. The relevance of these comments can be seen in four basic propositions that should be a part of any discussion of the self-evaluation process in any organization.

Four Basic Propositions

First, any institution, regardless of the original definition of purpose, whether it be a nation, a club, a private business or a local church, tends to turn in on itself and to become primarily concerned with survival and service to the members rather than with serving those who are not members of that institution. A nation is naturally more concerned with its citizens than with the welfare of "foreigners." A private business often puts the welfare of the stockholders above the needs of the clientele. A school tends to plan its schedule to suit the needs and convenience of the administration and faculty rather than the students. Likewise, a local church tends to plan its program to meet the needs, wants, and convenience of the members, and especially of the leaders, rather than those outside the congregation. This is not said critically, it is simply a description of a normal institutional tendency in any organization.

Second, every organization tends to move in the direction of redefining purpose in terms of institutional maintenance and survival. This pattern can be seen in both profit-oriented and nonprofit organizations, but it is especially prevalent in voluntary, nonprofit agencies. The care and feeding of the organization, rather than service to the clientele, tends to become the number one priority in the decision making process.

Third, any organization, but especially the voluntary nonprofit organization, that does not have tangible, highly visible, definable, and measurable goals tends to turn toward institutional maintenance as the primary concern of the organization.

Finally, any organization that places the primary emphasis on "pushing its product" rather than on meeting the needs of its clientele tends to go out of business. Whenever an organization becomes insensitive to the needs of people and concentrates instead on "doing business in the same old way," it begins to find itself in institutional jeopardy.

This can be seen in the retail store that refuses to adapt to new expectations by the customer in merchandising. It can be seen in the school that refuses to recognize the growing demand by students for the right of participation in the governing process. It can be seen in the local church where the Sunday school constitutes the entire program of Christian education. It can be seen in the college

95

where the lecture method of teaching still dominates the classroom style of the faculty. It can be seen in the local council of churches that still identifies its major responsibility as the training of church school teachers. It can be seen in the denominational agency that continues to develop and send out programs to be accepted and implemented by local churches.

Irrelevance is the term often applied to this condition.

What Are the Implications?

The parish leader who accepts the validity of these four propositions would be well advised to ponder their implications.

The most obvious implication is that when the members in a local church begin to list the questions and concerns they see confronting their church, there is a natural institutional pressure to emphasize problems growing out of institutional maintenance and frustration growing out of lack of clear sense of purpose—and these naturally tend to be identified in terms of persons and institutions rather than in terms of purpose, i.e. attack on the minister or on the parish church.

A second implication is that the local church needs to have a clear, cogent, internally consistent, highly visible, easily understood, widely accepted, and measurable definition of the purpose.

Furthermore, to meet these criteria, the members of the local church need to define and communicate to one another their sense of purpose as a congregation. It has to be "our" definition based on "our" understanding of the New Testament church.

It is not sufficient, however, simply to work out an acceptable statement of purpose. This statement of purpose must be translated into goals, objectives, and schedules if it is to be meaningful.

In addition, the congregation must have available to it the tools for evaluation that will enable it to measure how effectively it is achieving its goals and fulfilling its purpose. In this process of evaluation care must be exercised to make sure the tools of evaluation do measure accomplishment of purpose and do *not* subvert the definition of purpose. The usual annual report to the denomination and the typical committee report system seldom meet this need for evaluation and may subvert the process of implementation of purpose.

This means that any effort by a local church to use a definition of purpose as the focal point for its planning also should include evaluation as a part of the total process. Unless this is done, the whole process of defining purpose and setting goals may turn out to be an interesting but meaningless exercise.

It is possible to summarize what has been said thus far in one sentence. Unless a local church builds self-evaluation process into the life of that parish, it will be extremely vulnerable to normal institutional pressures to place a higher priority on survival than on service and to put institutional maintenance ahead of ministry in the allocation of resources.

This raises the question of how a congregation can build into its life an adequate self-evaluation process. A beginning of an answer to that question can be found in looking at four alternative approaches.

Four Approaches to Self-Evaluation

Old First Church is a 1,500 member congregation with a large and very beautiful sanctuary. The attendance at the one Sunday morning worship service is about 400 in the summer months, goes up to slightly over 500 during Lent, and averages 450 for the entire year.

The leaders decided to schedule a second worship service for each Sunday from the first of June through the middle of September. They thought that by adding an early service at 8:30 in the morning they might increase the summer attendance.

When asked whether they might continue two services during the rest of the year, the reply was, "We want to try it out first in the summer and see how it goes."

When pressed for details on how they will arrive at a determination on whether to go to two services on a year-round basis, the response was, "That will depend on how we feel about what happens with this summer's experiment."

When asked the specific question about how they would respond if the average attendance increased from the figure of 397 of the previous summer to an average of 410 for this coming summer, the responses varied. A few indicated that if this was the result, they would favor a continuation of the two worship service schedule. Others suggested that such a small increase would not justify continuing the early service. "After all," commented one layman, "if we would double the input of resources and have only a two or three percent increase in attendance, we would not win any awards for efficiency. Obviously you cannot justify that ratio of added input and increased output in any organization, even the church!"

In another city, two smaller congregations on opposite sides of the community also were concerned about the summer attendance slump. In both congregations the year-round attendance at worship averaged nearly 200, but dropped to 140 to 150 in the summer. Both congregations scheduled Thursday evening worship services in an attempt to serve the people who would be out of town over the weekend. In one congregation this special service had an attendance of 20 to 35 each week. The church council voted to discontinue it because of the low turnout.

In the other parish the Thursday evening attendance ranged between 15 and 35. The church council voted to continue it on a year-round basis on the grounds that this gave people a greater choice and more people participated in corporate worship each week because of this increased range of worship opportunities. In making the motion to continue the Thursday evening service, a layman explained his position by a reference to Matthew 18:20.

These examples illustrate one of the most common methods of self-evaluation employed in the local church. It is a very subjective response to events after they have occurred. This approach does not include advance objective expectations against which subsequent performance is measured.

A second approach is illustrated by the discussion that followed the treasurer's report at the annual meeting of a small, open-country church in rural Indiana. The treasurer concluded his report by stating, "We finished the year with a cash balance in the bank of $389.43. This is a decrease of over $121 from our balance at the end of last year. At this rate I figure this church can survive for another three to four years." The next twenty minutes were spent discussing whether the financial report, when considered with the contents of other reports, indicated a life expectancy of two or three or four years for this congregation.

Here, as in so many organizations, the central theme in the self-evaluation process was institutional survival. In this approach, survival rather than purpose becomes the yardstick for self-evaluation.

A third approach to self-evaluation can be found in many congregations where the questions asked in the annual report to the denomination constitute the agenda for self-evaluation.

While the number, the wording, and the format of the questions vary from denomination to denomination, in general the most that can be said is that for purposes of self-evaluation the questions asked in some denominations are even worse than in others. Most of the questions are concerned with the Sunday school, income and expenditures, property and organizations. Other than for a relatively few questions on baptisms, conversions, confirmations, weddings, and deaths, little is asked about people and what happened to the people in the parish.*

The number, wording, and mix of these questions tend to persuade the outsider that self-evaluation in the parish should focus on money and real estate rather than on people and their experiences.

This is not to suggest that questions on money and property are irrelevant, only that they are not always the most important or the most useful questions that should be raised in the self-evaluation process. The value of these questions for self-evaluation purposes is limited even further by the fact that

* For an excellent discussion of the quality of the questions asked by various denominations, see Samuel Southard "Second Chance For Church Records" in *Review of Religious Research*, X, Spring 1969, 180-85.

nearly always they are phrased to elicit a response only in absolute numbers rather than to encourage comparative analysis. It is useful to ask the average attendance at worship on Sunday morning. The value of this answer would be enhanced, however, if another question asked the ratio of worship attendance to confirmed membership. This would enable each congregation to compare its attendance ratio with that of the other congregations in that judicatory. Likewise, it is useful to ask the total giving for benevolences, but if another question asked for the ratio of benevolence giving to total giving, it would facilitate the self-evaluation process. In some denominations a step in this direction has been taken by reporting data on giving in both total amounts and on a per member basis. It is helpful to know how many persons transferred their membership into the parish and also how many transferred out. A question asking the net change by transfer would focus attention on these two trends and might provoke other questions in the self-evaluation effort.

Perhaps the most serious criticism of the majority of the questions in the annual report to the denomination, however, is that they may subvert the definition of purpose. Because they are asked, these questions may become the only questions on the agenda, and the leaders may conclude these questions reflect the purpose of the parish. It is an-easy step to move from these questions to the conclusion that the major purposes of the local church are to increase its membership, achieve a balanced budget, operate a large Sunday school, and carry an adequate amount of insurance on its property.

Perhaps the most creative approach to the self-evaluation effort is to first define purpose and formulate goals and objectives. After this has been accomplished, questions can be developed which keep the focus on performance rather than activity, on quality rather than quantity, on effectiveness rather than efficiency and economy, and on the basic purpose or end rather than on the means of achieving that end.

Now the question arises, How can a platitude such as that one be turned into some practical suggestions on improving the process of self-evaluation?

It is happening in scores of local churches and perhaps the most useful approach to that question is first to look briefly at how self-evaluation can be built into the parish planning process and then to review three specific approaches to improved self-evaluation.

Building in Self-Evaluation

When institutional survival becomes the primary goal in an organization, the only built-in answer to the natural question of "How are we doing?" is "We're still in business!"

In the organization that recognizes the value of self-evaluation as a means of appraising current performance, keeping the basic focus on the original definition of purpose and thus reducing the ravages of institutional blight, there must be some method of building into the normal administrative processes a format for self-evaluation. Unless this is done, the chances are very great that either there will be no meaningful self-evaluation or it will drift in the direction of questions on institutional maintenance, activities, and economy rather than on purpose, goals, and performance.

One approach to this subject in the local church is in the preparation of the general program goals for the congregation. Here a useful procedure is to follow this five-step process.

1. Relate the goal to the purpose of the church;
2. Define a programmatic means of implementing that goal;
3. Formulate a set of expectations;
4. Devise a method of evaluating direction and pace of movement in response to the goal;
5. Schedule, *in advance*, periodic review and evaluation.

This basic format can be adapted to a variety of situations to build in a process of self-evaluation. It can be used in planning a building program, in scheduling a second worship service, in establishing a meaningful climate for a new staff person, in developing a special program of visitation evangelism, in undertaking a new venture in weekday Christian education, or in launching a new ministry to meet a distinctive community need, such as a day-care center for the children of mothers employed outside the home.

Another approach to this need to build in a self-evaluation process is by focusing on the priority system that guides the decision-making process. Plymouth Church has a seven-year-old, twelve-room, Christian education building that is used for three hours on Sunday and is never used during the remaining 165 hours of the week. One of the members proposes the congregation sponsor a weekday nursery school for four- and five-year-old children and use several of the first floor rooms for this. In turning this proposal into a program, what are the considerations or the priorities that will guide the decision-making process?

　　To fill up those empty rooms?

　　To minister to members?

　　To serve non-members?

　　To plan program for people?

　　To enable the members of Plymouth Church to have another opportunity to be involved in ministry?

　　To hold down operating costs for Plymouth Church by getting some revenue for the use of those rooms?

Unless there can be some agreement on the ranking of these questions in terms of priorities, the new program probably will be a divisive force in that congregation. More important, unless there is some agreement on these priorities, it will be very difficult to evaluate the venture. If, however, a priority ranking can be assigned to these and similar questions, Plymouth Church will have a built-in basis for evaluating what has happened after six months.

A third approach to building in some form of self-evaluation is for a congregation to develop a generalized statement of criteria that will be used to evaluate every proposed alternative solution to every problem that comes before that congregation. In one parish a two-part form has been developed that is a part of the standard operating procedure in evaluating every alternative whenever this congregation reaches a fork in the road.

A. *General*

　　1. Which alternative will help us respond to the two or three most important concerns before us today?

2. What are the costs of each alternative?
   a. Dollars
   b. Manpower—paid and volunteer
   c. Elimination of other alternatives
3. Which will help us provide a diversified program and ministry to maximize our appeal to the maximum number of people?
4. Which will help us enlarge the base of participation in our program and ministry?
5. Which will leave the next generation of leaders with the maximum degree of flexibility?
6. Which is the most consistent with contemporary trends in parish developments? Which is most likely to be planning for tomorrow's needs rather than for yesterday's practices?

B. *Specific* (criteria that emerge from this specific question or problem)
   1.
   2.
   3.

By making this as much a part of the continuing administrative operation of the parish as the budget or the annual meeting, this congregation has built into the functioning of the church council a procedure for continuing self-evaluation.

The Annual Program Audit

"As I study the report of the nominating committee I see they have nominated someone to serve as church treasurer for the coming year, and they also have nominated an audit committee, to go over the treasurer's books at the end of the year," commented a twenty-six-year-old member during the annual congregational meeting at Pilgrim Church.

"Now the heart of my question is this, Mr. Moderator, what is important around here? We are going to elect three people to audit or review the treasurer's records to make sure that job has been done properly, but I don't see anyone being nominated to review or examine or audit the work of the different program committees, such as education, worship, evangelism, and social action. Why not? Aren't they important?"

"I'm not sure I understand your question," responded the moderator after a long pause, "but I guess we who are here as the participants in this annual meeting constitute a review committee. During the course of this meeting we hear and act on the reports of all the boards and committees of this church. Therefore, it seems to me we don't need to nominate any committee to review the reports of the boards and committees. That's what we're here for this evening."

"You're missing my point," persisted the young member who had not even been born when the present moderator had first been elected to a leadership position at Pilgrim Church. "We already have heard and approved the treasurer's report today, but we still are going to elect a committee to carefully review the treasurer's books to make sure everything is in order. What I hear you saying is that we trust the program committees to review and report on the quality of their work, but we don't trust the treasurer to report on the quality of her work. Why not? Is the work of the evangelism committee so unimportant that we don't bother asking anyone to review their work, but the work of the treasurer is so important that we need a careful outside audit?"

"I'm afraid you don't understand business

106

practices," replied the moderator who was becoming somewhat exasperated. "It's simply a good business practice to audit the treasurer's books once a year. If we didn't do this annually, and if we happened to have an inept treasurer, it might take months or years to get everything straightened out again."

"Now we're communicating," replied the questioner eagerly. "We are in agreement! We need to apply good business practices to the operation of Pilgrim Church. Our business is ministry and we need to be sure we're doing our business properly. Let me pick up the point you just made. Suppose we happen to have an inept education committee or an inept evangelism committee, if we don't audit their work annually it might take months or years to get everything straightened out again. Just as we can't take the risk of depending on the church treasurer to evaluate the quality of her bookkeeping, we can't risk letting the program committee evaluate the quality of their performance."

"This is a very provocative discussion," interrupted the chairman of the nominating committee, "but frankly I don't know what instructions we would give a program review committee if we elected one. We know how you audit the treasurer's books, but how do you audit the work of the evangelism committee?"

This discussion introduces one of the most creative evaluation procedures available to the local church. This is the annual program review. The typical application of this concept in the local church involves five steps.

1. For each program committee in the parish there is a written "job description" that includes the purpose and responsibilities of that committee and its relationship to the total organization of the parish.

This may be taken from the denominational manual or it may be custom tailored by that congregation for its own unique circumstances.

2. Each committee is asked to describe how its purpose relates to the central purpose and the overall goals of that congregation and to the work and responsibilities of the other program committees.

3. Each year each committee is asked to carefully formulate for the coming year its general goals, its specific objectives, the program it is planning to implement, the schedule for achieving these objectives, and the means by which it is going to evaluate its progress during the coming year.

4. This comprehensive statement must be prepared and submitted to the special program review committee by the first of the year. In effect, each program committee says, "This is what we plan to do during the next twelve months, this is how we plan to do it, and this is how you can evaluate our progress."

5. Just as it does with the treasurer's responsibilities, each year the congregation receives two reports on each program area. One is from the program committee. The other is from the program review committee that evaluates the total program of the parish as well as the work of each separate committee.

The most obvious disadvantage of this evaluation procedure is that it means considerable work for many people.

The congregations that have used this type of self-evaluation procedure usually report, however, that the benefits greatly exceed the cost in time and energy. Among the advantages reported are these six.

The first advantage is directly related to the central thesis of this chapter. This approach to self-evaluation tends to put the focus on purpose, goals, program, and performance instead of institutional maintenance. This is true not only at the annual meeting, but throughout the year.

A second value is that this structures into the life of the congregation a requirement for reflection on purpose, a discussion of goals, and decisions on program that are consistent with purpose and goals.

Closely related to this, and at least equally important, is the fact that this approach to evaluation forces each program committee to formulate its own goals and objectives rather than being charged with implementing some other person's or committee's ideas. As each committee sets its own goals and schedules in advance, and as each one develops the standards by which its work will be evaluated, this tends to have a very favorable impact on the performance of that program committee.

A fourth benefit from this approach is that it encourages a holistic approach to the life, ministry, and program of the parish. Each program committee is asked to look at its purpose and responsibilities in relationship to the total program of that congregation. In its work, the program review committee evaluates the work of each separate program committee from the perspective of that committee's goals and also from an overall view of the mission of that congregation.

In addition, this procedure almost invariably produces a tremendous improvement in the quality of the reporting. In their annual reports, parish program committees tend to follow one of two approaches. Some simply fill out the form provided by the denomination, usually wondering why there are so many irrelevant questions on the form, and that is their annual report. The other is to provide a narrative account of meetings, activities, and similar items. The use of the annual program review provides a frame of reference built around purpose, relationships, goals, expectations, schedules, and accomplishments. This means the annual report of that program committee tends to compare actual performance with earlier expectations. This is the best approach to making the reporting system a useful part of the self-evaluation process.

Finally, a few congregations have added a refinement to the annual program review that provides some interesting fringe benefits. They do this by exchanging review committees. The program review committee from Plymouth Church examines the work of the program committees at St. Paul's Church, while the committee from St. Paul's reviews the work of the committees at Calvary Church, and the review committee from Calvary goes to Plymouth Church.

This refinement adds a new perspective to the review process in each congregation, it opens the door to the "vision and model" concept of introducing new ideas into a local church that is referred to in the latter part of chapter 3; it reduces the possibility that personality clashes or ancient rivalries will disrupt the annual program review; and it creates a new possibility for meaningful intercongregational cooperation on program. In addition, in at least two cases, it has added a new excitement to the annual meeting!

Asking Better Questions

The nature of the questions asked in the reporting system affect the performance of the organization.

This is one of the most significant findings that has emerged from recent research in the procedures and methods of evaluation. This means the questions are more important than the answers in influencing the performance of an organization. Or, to be more specific, it suggests that since the questions influence a parish's definition of its purpose, it should evaluate the quality and significance of the questions that are asked. Earlier in this chapter it was suggested that the questions asked in the reporting by local churches to the denominational agencies tend to be less than outstanding in quality and usefulness. Since these questions often are the only questions a congregation asks itself, they tend not only to provide the only basis for both external evaluation and internal evaluation, they also affect the understanding of mission and the ordering of priorities.

What are some better questions?

The answer should be on a congregation by congregation basis, in which the questions are custom tailored to the type, role, purpose, mission, and program of each congregation. It is possible, however, to suggest questions that both illustrate the central point of this section and also have proved to be helpful in the self-evaluation process in congregations of various types.

In addition to asking for the total confirmed membership and the average attendance at corporate worship, ask "How many members attended at least once during an average month such as October or May?"

In addition to asking how many corporate worship services were conducted last year, ask "How many different opportunities for corporate worship were available to the membership?"

111

In addition to asking how many people attended corporate worship in this parish last year, ask "How many different people had an active role in planning and leading corporate worship last year?"

In addition to asking how many persons joined this congregation last year, ask "What happened to them because they joined this church?"

In addition to asking how many members were removed from the membership roll by action of the governing body of the congregation during the past five years, ask "What proportion of those removed joined this congregation by letter of transfer and what proportion joined by confession of faith or confirmation?"; "How does that proportion compare to the proportion of all confirmed members who joined this congregation by letter of transfer?"

In addition to asking for the average attendance in the church school, ask "What happened to the people who attended our church school regularly?"

In addition to asking about the structure, the number of classes and the enrollment in the church school, ask "What are the presuppositions and assumptions on which our whole program of Christian education is based?"

In addition to asking the number of children enrolled in the nursery and kindergarten classes ask "Is the style of teaching based on the needs of the children or the wants and convenience of the teachers?" Or, better yet, "Does the pedagogical style used follow David C. Cook or Sesame Street? Which is the more appropriate?"

In addition to asking for the value, the indebtedness, and the amount of the insurance on the church property, ask "How is this property being used in mission and ministry?"

112

In addition to asking for the total expenditures by this congregation for the past year, ask "How much was spent to maintain the property and how much was spent in ministry to people?"

In addition to asking what proportion of the total congregational receipts were "sent away" as benevolence giving for the work of the larger church, ask "What proportion of the total congregational receipts were used for mission and ministry in *this* community to people outside the membership of the parish?"

In addition to asking each program committee to report on their activities for the past year, ask "What did you as a committee learn during the past year that will enable you to carry out your responsibilities more effectively next year?"

In addition to asking the number of professional staff members employed by the congregation, ask "What proportion of each one's time is spent carrying out our ministry for us and what proportion is spent enabling the members to respond to their call to ministry and service?"

In addition to asking the amount of money required for any proposed new program, project, or ministry, ask "What values will be enhanced or what goals will be achieved by the approval of this request?"

In addition to asking about any new programs or ministries that were added during the past year, ask "What programs or ministries that have become obsolete or irrelevant were terminated during the past year?"

Other suggestions for useful self-evaluation questions can be found in the section "The Self-Renewing

113

Congregation" in chapter 3, and "What Makes a Difference" in chapter 5.

After these and similar questions have been asked and answered by the evaluation committee in your parish, if the members of the parish evaluation committee ask, "Of what value is this material?" the time has come to add one more question to the list. Do we need a new self-evaluation committee in this parish?

The Question of Accountability

"All of this talk about the lines of accountability is unnecessary. This is not like the typical business arrangement where you have to accept the problem of irresponsibility as a fact of life. Here you have committed Christians who are trying to respond to the call of the Lord in faithfulness and obedience. They will do what is right without a lot of elaborate safeguards. After all, each one realizes he is accountable to God. That's enough to keep him on the right track!"

This comment represents the traditional response of many churchmen when the question of accountability is raised. In most ecclesiastical organizations the lines of accountability are grossly inadequate. This is true of the typical local church, of most denominational agencies, of theological seminaries, of nearly all interdenominational organizations, of a great many specialized ministries, and of a good share of the church-sponsored social welfare agencies.

Despite this glaring inadequacy, there is a widespread inclination to assume that since all church leaders mean well it is unnecessary to establish clearly defined lines of accountability in ecclesiastical organizations.

114

That response is unrealistic. A specialized ministry in a large wealthy, eastern, suburban community ran up a deficit of over a half million dollars in a matter of months because of inadequate lines of accountability.

That response is unbiblical. It runs counter to the biblical concept of stewardship.

That response is vulnerable theologically. It overlooks the doctrine of original sin.

That response is administrative nonsense. It neglects the distinction between intent and action, between honesty and responsibility, and between commitment and competence.

That response is institutionally naïve. It ignores the fact that an inadequate system of accountability is one of the leading causes of institutional blight in an organization.

That response is a major barrier to any attempt at continuing self-evaluation. Unless individuals and organizations are held accountable for their performance, it is impossible to develop a system of self-evaluation, and if it could be developed, it would be valueless.

The importance of accountability as a factor in improving the quality of performance in an organization, in reducing morale problems among the members or employees, and in countering the ravages of institutional blight is receiving increasing attention in management circles. An adequate system of accountability is being recognized as essential if the process of self-evaluation is to be meaningful. As the size and complexity of the organization increases, the value of clear lines of accountability grows.

Within the churches increasing attention is being given to a dozen aspects of this subject.

1. To whom is the pastor accountable for his performance? The congregation? A congregational committee? If so, which one? Pastor-parish relations? The finance committee? The governing board of the congregation? The lay leader? A denominational executive? Himself? God?

2. In a congregation with two or more professional staff members, to whom is the associate minister accountable? To whom is the director of music accountable? The church business administrator? Who evaluates the work of each professional staff member? When? On what basis?

3. To whom are the lay leaders of the congregation accountable? Who evaluates their performance? When? On what basis?

4. Within the parish, what are the lines of accountability among the several boards and committees? In many congregations the trustees have been the major power center. Should the program committee be administratively responsible to the trustees? Or should the trustees be responsible to the central program committee? This is a basic question, since the answer indicates whether the building is being operated to house program or whether the primary purpose of the congregation is to maintain the building.

5. What is the accountability of an elected board to the group that elected it, especially if that group meets only once every two or three or four years?

6. What are the lines of accountability of the

denominational staff? In fact, do they implement policy or do they make policy?

7. What are the lines of accountability when several denominational staff persons are employed within the same judicatory, each with his own "supervisory" board or committee?

8. What are the lines of accountability from the denominational judicatory to the congregation? The lines of accountability are relatively well established in the opposite direction.

9. What is the place of finances in the accountability process—do the lines of accountability follow the organizational chart or the funding process? When these are separate, what happens?

10. Do the churches have obligations to society? If so, what are the lines of accountability?

11. When an ecclesiastical agency is funded by one group to provide a service ministry to another constituency, which is the *primary* line of accountability? To the sources of the funds? To the clientele?

12. What is the relationship between the principles of representative government in the churches and the lines of accountability?

There are no simple answers to most of these questions. There are few answers that can be applied universally. Basically, each organization has to work out the answers appropriate to it as it struggles with the question of accountability. Unless these questions are answered, however, it will be difficult to combat institutional blight, it will be almost impossible to develop a useful process of self-evaluation, it will be difficult to plan effectively, and it will make any

117

discussion about improving the implementation of limited value.

SUGGESTIONS FOR FURTHER READING

Bauer, Raymond A., ed. *Social Indicators*. Cambridge, Mass.: M.I.T. Press, 1966.

Churchman, C. West. *The Systems Approach*. New York: Dell Books, 1968.

Department of Health, Education and Welfare. *Toward a Social Report*. Washington: U.S. Government Printing Office, 1969.

Gross, Bertram M. *Organizations and Their Managing*. New York: The Free Press, 1968.

Levitt, Theodore. *The Marketing Mode*. New York: McGraw-Hill, 1969.

Lindgren, Alvin J. *Foundations for Purposeful Church Administration*. Nashville: Abingdon Press, 1965.

Report of the Special Commission on the Social Sciences of the National Science Board. *Knowledge Into Action: Improving the Nation's Use of the Social Sciences*. Washington: U.S. Government Printing Office, 1969.

Schaller, Lyle E. "The Call For Evaluation." *Church Management*, April 1969.

Schaller, Lyle E. *The Impact of the Future*. Nashville: Abingdon Press, 1969.

Schein, Edgar H. *Process Consultation: Its Role in Organization Development*. Reading, Mass.: Addison-Wesley Publishing Co., 1969.

5
GETTING FROM HERE TO THERE

"The effective parish pastor can do four things," commented a veteran denominational executive at a meeting in Texas. "He can help the members of a congregation discover who they are, where they are now, where they should be, and how to get from where they are now to where they should be."

This is a simple summary of one man's definition of the role of the parish pastor, but the limitations of this statement were quickly revealed by the response of a minister who was present at that meeting. "I believe our people know what the church is, we certainly know where we are now, and we have a pretty good idea of where we should be," he said. "What we need is help in getting from where we are to where we should be. We have a statement of purpose, a program, and a set of goals. Now how do we go about fulfilling our statement of purpose, reaching our goals, and implementing our plan?"

In his brief comments, this pastor raised one of the basic questions in parish planning. He also gave the first part of the answer. The question is—How does a parish implement its plans? How does it get from here to there?

Six Essential Elements in the Implementation Process

The first part of the answer is in deciding where to go or what to do. In his remarkable book on how organizations function, *Innovation in Marketing,* Theodore Levitt wrote, "Unless you know where you're going, any road will take you there."

The second basic step in implementing any plan is to determine what is possible. There is a romantic ring to such phrases as "the courage to fail" or "the world writes the agenda for the church" or Daniel Burnham's famous "Make no little plans; they have no magic to stir men's blood and probably themselves will not be realized. Make big plans." However, these phrases have a very limited utility when the process reaches the implementation stage. In the vast majority of cases, it is important to examine the proposed plan for its feasibility. Are the current and potential resources adequate for the task? Is this a project this congregation can carry through? What will be the probable consequences of failure?

A church leader living in New York City picks up five pieces of paper from the sidewalk every day. He says this is the only way he can continue to live there without surrendering to the clutter of the environment. He calls this "the limited agenda of the possible."

Likewise, few congregations can solve the problem of poverty by themselves, or eliminate racial injustice, or bring an end to war. Each one can, however, take responsibility for a piece of such problems if they can prepare their own "agenda of the possible."

When a congregation is challenged with a task of manageable proportions, it often will respond affirmatively. Too often, however, a congregation is

120

charged with global tasks such as ending war or eliminating the last traces of racial injustice or overcoming the generation gap. When they are left without even a handle to grasp in taking hold of such mammoth problems, the members are left feeling impotent, frustrated, and guilty; feelings which may later turn into outrage.

In writing the agenda of the possible, there are two potential pitfalls to be avoided. The most common of these is to mistake politeness for agreement. People have a natural tendency to avoid disagreement or unpleasantness and nowhere is this more prevalent than in the local church. More than one pastor has made the mistake of assuming that the members agreed with him and supported his views and plans, when, in fact, they were only being polite.

The second pitfall is the temptation to overload the agenda. In most, but not all situations the agenda of the possible has only one item on it at any one time. Rarely do the available resources of the local church permit the luxury of undertaking two or three or four *new* or additional ministries at any one point in history. Usually it is wiser to elect a one-at-a-time approach. A few congregations, for example, have a self-defined schedule that calls for launching one new program or ministry each year. In five years, this approach can revitalize the life of a parish. Sometimes it is helpful to broaden this approach to launching one new program every year and also *to terminating one obsolete or irrelevant program each year.* This dual thrust is useful in small congregations where resources are limited, in older congregations where precedent is powerful, and in larger congregations where inertia enables obsolete programs to continue long after they have outlived their usefulness.

121

A third part of the implementation process is to translate hopes, plans, and general goals into operational objectives. There is a difference between the general goal of "providing a helpful physical setting for corporate worship" and a plan for remodeling the chancel. There is a difference between the general goal of "spreading the good news of Jesus Christ" and the operational or specific goal of receiving sixty new members on profession of faith next year. There is a difference between "helping to eliminate hunger" and allocating ten percent of the proceeds from the capital funds drive for a breakfast program in Chicago's near south side.

It is impossible to overemphasize the crucial importance of operational goals. A simple illustration of this point can be seen in the eighty-member rural congregation meeting in a small white frame building by the side of a blacktop road in the open country. Behind the church is a hundred-year-old cemetery.

This congregation hears two voices, both emphasizing purpose and goals. The first voice declares the church is the body of Christ and the goal of this congregation must be to make the love of God in Christ manifest in this community.

The second voice says the purpose of this congregation is to maintain this cemetery and the specific goals for the coming year are (a) replace the fence on the west side of the cemetery, (b) keep the grass cut, and (c) make sure the income at least matches the expenditures.

Which of these two voices will be heard *and acted upon by the members of that congregation?*

In translating general goals into specific operational objectives, it is absolutely essential that each specific objective be examined very carefully to make sure it

122

is consistent with the basic definition of purpose. It is remarkably easy for the message to be garbled in the translation process. One congregation set for itself the general goal of "strengthening our ministry of Christian education and nurture." One of the operational objectives that was defined after months of study was to "phase out the three-hour after-school program for fifth and sixth graders on Wednesday afternoons, since over ninety percent of the participants also attend Sunday school at least two Sundays a month." In translating general goals into operational objectives, economy had replaced performance as one of the criteria.

This part of the implementation process often is referred to as "management by objective" in business circles, and several elements of this concept merit the attention of local church leaders. Five of the essential elements in management by objective are defining the target, mobilizing the necessary resources, laying out a schedule, identifying the checkpoints or mileposts for periodic measurements of progress, and developing a system of evaluation for self-correction and reporting. The usefulness of each of these steps is illustrated very clearly in a building program. They are equally useful in developing an adult study program, in carrying out a plan of visitation evangelism, and in implementing a ministry to the high school drug scene.

Another essential element in implementation is timing. "For everything there is a season, and a time for every matter under heaven" is the opening verse of a widely quoted chapter in the book of Ecclesiastes. It is the inspiration of a popular folk song. It is also good advice to the parish leader who has a proposal he would like to see adopted in his local

123

church. November may not be the appropriate time
to try to implement a radical restructuring of the
church school. The last three months before his retirement may not be the appropriate time for a pastor
to urge a revision of the Sunday morning schedule.
The long delayed plan to open a day-care center
probably should not be implemented in the same
month that St. James Church, a block away, is opening their new day-care center for the children of working mothers.

An Indiana pastor illustrated the importance of
timing in most colorful language. It's like a boy and
girl planning to take a romantic walk in the moon-
light, and one says, "If you get there first, go right
on, don't wait for me."

A fifth factor that should be considered by anyone
interested in a systematic approach to the implementation process is the point of intervention. Any new
idea or change requires a breaking into the continuity
of the traditional patterns of life in the parish.

This can be seen by looking at long established
congregations where the physical environment sur-
rounding the meeting place is undergoing rapid
change. This may be old First Church in the central
business district of a large city, it may be a small
rural church, it may be an inner-city church, or it
may be a sixty-year-old suburban congregation.

As the neighborhood changes from what the members perceived as a friendly environment to what
many eventually will describe as a hostile environment, many of these individual members go through
a recognition process that includes these steps.

1. Unawareness of changes
2. Limited awareness
3. Greater awareness and increasing apprehension

about the impact of these changes on "our" church
4. Apprehension turns into fear
5. Fears recognized
6. Gradual increase in openness and willingness to talk about what is happening

The dominant response of the local church to change during the first four steps of this process is silence.

At that point in the process when many of the members are in the third or fourth or fifth stages, other members may be in the first or second or sixth stage. A congregation going through this process resembles a long parade (pilgrimage) passing an intersection rather than an automobile going down the road where its exact location at any one point in time can be pinpointed precisely.

This is an important point to remember, especially for the person in the sixth stage of process. The first persons to arrive at this sixth stage tend to assume everyone is where they are and often insist on limiting the discussion to "What are we going to do about it?"

A far more constructive approach for these persons to take is to walk back along side the pilgrimage and help the other members reach that point in their response to change where they feel ready to talk about what is happening. When many of the leaders and most of the members are in the early and middle stages of this process, any action proposal (except in a time of genuine crisis) is likely to be greeted by silence, a look of incomprehension, hostility, or spontaneous rejection.

Little will be achieved by asking people to respond *thoughtfully* to a problem until after they have recog-

125

nized the existence of the problem, recovered from their initial fears, and developed an openness to discuss what is happening.

The same pattern can be seen in efforts at interchurch cooperation between parishes. Trinity and Calvary are similar type congregations in the same neighborhood. Nearly all of the leaders and most of the members at Calvary are in the sixth stage of the process described earlier. They conclude that one of the most attractive action alternatives is a cooperative ministry with Trinity Church. A committee from Calvary goes to meet with the leaders of Trinity and present the proposal for a cooperative ministry.

Most of the leaders and nearly all of the members at Trinity are scattered along the first three steps of this process. They have great difficulty as they try to grasp what it is the people from Calvary are saying and why they are making this proposal and, therefore, are polite but noncommittal.

Eventually the Calvary delegation goes home, completely convinced that Trinity is simply an uncooperative congregation. The lesson they should have learned is that the introduction of an action proposal into the process before the leaders reach the last step in this sequence usually is unproductive and occasionally may be either counterproductive or destructive.

Among the most helpful methods that have been used in helping people move more rapidly to the open discussion stage are these five:

1. A twenty-four to forty-eight-hour retreat involving four to six leaders from each of four to six congregations in similar situations.

2. A visit by leaders of one or more parishes to parishes in similar situations *that have re-*

sponded creatively to similar changes and challenges in other cities.
3. A twelve to twenty-four-hour training event involving leaders from several parishes currently involved in an affirmative response to change—perhaps two hours an evening for several evenings.
4. A congregational self-study.
5. Participation by parish leaders in a low-key high-trust type of encounter group.

There are two other points of possible intervention that have proved their value. The first of these is the budgeting process. (See chapter 2 for a detailed discussion of this point.) Frequently the preparation of the parish budget offers an opportunity for introducing a new idea or bringing up a proposal that has been discussed but never implemented. If a sum of money is appropriated for implementing a program, the adoption of the budget constitutes an official approval of the proposal. In addition, putting it in the budget often means there will be some form of periodic evaluation of the progress that has been made in implementing the proposal.

An excellent example of this is the proposal to provide opportunities for specialized training for laymen. In some congregations this idea floated around for years with a vague, general approval, but never was implemented. When an item was included in the budget—typically one percent of the total local budget—this provided the basis for (a) official approval, (b) funds for implementation, and (c) a monthly reminder of the proposal as the treasurer presented the financial report for the previous month. If, by October, nothing had been expended from this account, someone might ask, "How come

127

nothing has been done about this matter of inservice training for laymen? If we thought the idea had sufficient merit to be included in the budget last fall, why has nothing been done to provide training opportunities or to encourage people to go to workshops and seminars?"

The other possible point of intervention that should not be overlooked is discontent. Whenever people are discontented with the present situation, the opportunity is present to begin the process of planned social change. More will be said on this subject later in this chapter, but discontent, whether it is caused by a simple problem or a major crisis, often provides the most creative point of intervention in the process of implementing new ideas in the parish.

A sixth essential element in the implementation process, and perhaps the one that is most often neglected, can be summarized in the one word, *participation.*

One of the most common practices in many organizations is for one person or group to study a problem, come up with a proposed course of action, have it approved and then delegate the responsibility for implementation to another person or group.

One of the most common complaints in many organizations is "We seem to be always hearing reports of special studies, adopting resolutions, and approving new programs, but nothing ever happens. These reports, resolutions, and proposed programs rarely are implemented."

These two paragraphs explain why the implementation process breaks down so frequently in voluntary associations. The obvious answer is to involve the persons who will be responsible for implementation of the program in planning and preparation of the program. Very few persons are interested in helping to implement anything other than good ideas of meritorious programs. Every person's definition of a good idea or of a meritorious program is one which was either his idea or one which he helped formulate.

In any action program, the persons responsible for its implementation should participate in the development of the program.

In addition to these six essential elements in the implementation process, there are several other factors that deserve a more extensive analysis. Possibly the most important of these in the local church is the matter of expectations.

The Importance of Expectations

"The little brown envelope in the bulletin this morning is for a special offering for the victims of hurricane Camille that caused so much damage along the coast of Mississippi three weeks ago. You are each asked to use this envelope if you would like to share in this special appeal." This was one of three announcements made by a pastor during a worship service one September morning.

When the persons responsible for counting the offering spilled the contents of the collection plates out on a table later that morning, they found a total of 352 little brown envelopes. When they were opened they found a dollar in each of 349, one had a five-dollar bill, and the other two each contained a ten-dollar bill. One person commented that apparently three individuals found themselves without a dollar bill when they came to church that morning.

In another church on that same morning, a similar announcement was made by the pastor, but he

129

added these two sentences "We do not receive a special offering in this parish unless it has been considered and approved by our Council on Ministries. They have studied this proposed appeal, they have approved it, and they have set a target of $1,500 as the appropriate goal as we respond to this appeal."

When the offering plates were emptied that morning, there were 337 little brown envelopes mixed in with the rest of the collection. These 337 envelopes contained a total of $1,577.

These two congregations were similar in nearly all respects, including size, income of the members, budgets, past history, and level of giving. The one big difference was that in the second congregation a goal was set, the persons present were given a target to aim for, and when those churchgoers heard the appeal described, they knew what was expected. They were told that the appeal had been approved or "legitimatized" and it was obvious to everyone present that many people would have to respond with a five-, ten-, or twenty-dollar bill if the goal was to be achieved.

In the first congregation, there was no articulation of any expectation beyond the appeal to put something in the brown envelope. In today's American culture, society has set the norm for a "decent" response to any appeal for funds. This is a dollar bill.

In the first congregation, the leadership did not articulate any expectations of the members. In the second, the leadership did. The difference in the response illustrates the significance of expectations. This is one of the most important lessons to be examined in studying the implementation process in church planning. Expectations make a difference!

The behavioral scientists have much to say to

church leaders. They have found that behavior is a product of many forces including drives, needs, expectations, external demands, past experiences, and the capacity of people to deal with these forces.

Experts on child care, industrial psychologists, administrators, parents and natural leaders all concur on one point. The simplest way to activate (persuade) someone is to expect that he will behave in a certain manner.

The pastor of a new Lutheran mission was describing how he had made over six hundred consecutive census calls in a new subdivision without once being turned down. A Presbyterian minister challenged him by saying, "That's hard to believe! Three months ago my associate went out into that very same neighborhood to call, and at least a third of the houses the person who came to the door wouldn't even give him the time of day much less talk about the church affiliations. How did you do it?"

The Lutheran pastor's response was simple. "I expected everyone to be cooperative and they were. Oh, once in a while, someone would start to refuse to answer my questions and I would reply, 'Oh come now, you're not going to turn me down are you? This is the two hundred and seventh house I've called at and no one has turned me down yet, you aren't going to be the first are you?' I must admit," he added, "that at the six hundred and seventeenth house, the woman simply said 'yes' and closed the door."

The influence and importance of expectations are recognized in many different ways by able leaders. After his fourth year, the pastor of an Ohio congregation included these two paragraphs in his report to the members:

131

"I must confess that after four years it seems to me at times that little has been accomplished. Changes come slowly in a large church like ours and not nearly as dramatically as in suburban areas where everything is new.

"Three things, however, are of paramount importance: (1) We are blessed with an abundance of dedicated and able laymen. One of our greatest problems is harnessing the talent we already have! (2) I am convinced the life of our church is moving in the right direction. There is a genuine and exciting hunger for renewal based on a strong desire both to know the faith and to witness more effectively to it. Along with this spiritual impetus is a healthy impatience to get on with the building program so long overdue. I predict that next year will be our year to rebuild. (3) I am also convinced that the best years for this congregation are still ahead. It is this vision of a more vital church, witnessing with increasing power to the claims of the Christian Gospel in our community and in the world, that is the greatest challenge of all."

He was articulating an affirmative set of expectations about the quality of lay leadership in that congregation, about the quality of life in that gathered community, and about the future.

Five final comments need to be made about the place and value of expectations in church planning.

First, the most influential expectations are those that are widely shared. It is helpful if the leaders have high, affirmative expectations. It is more likely, however, that these expectations will be fulfilled if they are widely shared among the members.

Second, expectations are conditioned by past experiences. The folk saying "success breeds success" represents an accumulation of wisdom about life.

Third, once an expectation has been articulated, it is important to follow up with some form of measurement or accountability or reporting. It greatly impairs results, adversely affects future response, and hurts morale unless this is done. In the second congregation described at the beginning of this section, four reports were made to the members on the response to the special appeal. It was reported in the weekly church newsletter, it was in the church bulletin on the following Sunday, the pastor mentioned it in his announcements from the pulpit, and it was reported to the meetings of the administrative board, the council on ministries, and the commission on missions.

Fourth, one of the major sources of tensions in congregations is that too few recognize the conflict that can be created by the tension between naïve and unrealistic expectations and the reality of organizational life. Examples of this abound. The list includes the young seminary graduate, with a vision of what the church should be and great expectations for his first parish, who is disillusioned when he finds the members behaving like human beings and the parish having several forms of institutional blight. It includes a man like John F. Kennedy, who expected the power of the presidency to be far greater than it turned out to be. It includes the members of the local church who expected a new building would solve all of their Sunday school problems. The list includes the congregation who thought a change of pastors would eliminate all of the problems, and it includes the pastor who expected a change of parishes would greatly improve his ministry.

Unless what is sometimes called "the zest of ambiguity" is recognized, too heavy reliance on the in-

133

fluence of expectations can produce frustrations rather than achievement.

Finally, the articulation of expectations must be accompanied by "handles" or operational goals the people can grasp. Again, the opening illustration in this section provides an instructive example. Instead of a very general statement such as "We expect this parish to respond to the crisis produced by the hurricane," the second congregation was offered a specific means of responding and this was accompanied by a challenging goal that was within reach. As goals are achieved, the "reach" of the congregation often grows and previously unattainable targets come into range.

While it is difficult to overemphasize the importance of expectations in the implementation process, the value of expectations is dependent upon the quality of communication within the parish. This brings up a subject in which the assumptions often do not coincide with reality.

Five Safe Assumptions in Communications

"If I had only known that you were planning to do this, Pastor, I would have been able to help," apologized Mrs. Wright as she lamented her failure to participate in a special ministry the church had recently undertaken.

As he listened to Mrs. Wright's apologies, the pastor was mentally recounting the number of opportunities this very loyal church member had had to hear about this venture. It had been announced twice from the pulpit, there had been a two-line mention of it in the bulletin, the monthly church newsletter had carried a three-paragraph description with a plea for volunteers, and it had been discussed at length in church council. The pastor assumed that since the message had been sent at least five times it should have been received.

This was a misleading assumption and one which frequently causes a breakdown in the implementation process. There are five assumptions about communications that merit the serious consideration of anyone interested in moving from ideas to action or in turning proposals into programs, and this episode illustrates the most critical of the five.

The first assumption about communication, and the only safe assumption, is that *the message did not get through to the intended recipient*. The person who always assumes the opposite is guaranteed disappointment and frustration.

Based upon what is happening in the rest of society, it appears that at least seventy percent of all the messages that are transmitted in the typical parish are not received. That percentage is rising every year.

The most widespread response to this condition is to increase the degree of redundancy. Through duplication, repetition, and overlap, the sender hopes to get his message through to the intended recipient. Normally, the more important the message to the sender (but not necessarily to the receiver), the greater the degree of redundancy. This explains why the six-year-old repeats himself so often as he attempts to interrupt the family conversation at the table. Instinctively he knows he is competing with others in a heavily overloaded communications network. (For an elaboration of this point see chapter 8.)

The second assumption about communication that is critical to the implementation process is that *if the message did get through, it was garbled in the process of transmission.* Sometimes it was an error in the transmission. Thus, when July 26 falls on a Tuesday, the postcard notice of the meeting may read "Monday, July 26." Sometimes the error is at the point of receipt of the message. The notice is printed correctly, but the reader "sees" Monday, July 26.

Just as many messages are sent that are never received, so there are many messages that are received that were never sent.

The reader has already encountered an example of this in the discussion of innovation in chapter 3. The four T's of trust, time, talk, and tolerance were being discussed in a seminar of ten denominational executives when a black district superintendent pointed out that he was not receiving the same message the others thought was being transmitted.

"I hear you talking about trust, time, talk, and tolerance as necessary ingredients in the process of introducing new ideas into an organization," he said. "I am sure you white men have no trouble understanding the logic of this. I am sure you all see trust, time, talk, and tolerance as essential elements in any effort at progress. Now let me tell you what a black man hears when he hears those four words.

"When you say 'trust,' I hear white men saying they will be willing to grant Negroes equality after we prove we can be trusted.

"When you say 'time,' I hear white men telling me and my children to be patient, that it takes time to reach full equality, and besides, look at how much progress has been made in just fifteen years!

"When you say 'talk,' I hear white men telling us black people to sit down and talk it over when we demand full equality now. When you say we need to be willing to take time to talk about it, I hear you saying you are not interested in *any* change now.

"When you say 'tolerance,' I begin to lose my cool. I've been tolerated in the church for too long, I would like to be accepted, not simply tolerated!"

The ten white men present learned two lessons that day. One was a lesson in how to look at the world from another man's perspective. The other was that the message that is received is not always the message that was sent. Perhaps the two lessons have considerable overlap.

The third assumption that deserves attention in the implementation process is that *an acknowledgment of receipt of the message does not necessarily imply approval or acceptance of the contents.*

"I can't understand why Bill isn't here. It's now eight-thirty and when I told him about the meeting he looked me right in the eye and repeated back to me, 'Tuesday night at the church, eight o'clock'; he should be walking in the door any minute now," said the chairman of the finance committee at the Pine Street Baptist Church as they anxiously awaited the arrival of one of the key members.

Two hours later, when it became apparent that Bill was not going to appear, the chairman understood a little more clearly the distinction between the acknowledgment of the receipt of the message and the acceptance of the contents.

There are many different levels of response to messages that are transmitted in the parish and clearly are being received by members of the congregation. These include receipt, acceptance, approval, and commitment. The existence of these several levels is a common cause of misunderstanding, confusion, and other malfunctions that inhibit the implementation process.

"Will you come to the meeting at the church Tuesday night?" "Yes" is the response. The person extending the invitation may assume the "yes" means receipt, approval, acceptance, and commitment. The person making the response may be only acknowledging receipt of the invitation or he may be committing himself to attend.

"Will you come to the meeting at the church and bring the refreshments?" This probably is a much clearer message since it asks for a commitment. If the listener heard both halves of this message and responded affirmatively, this response probably is at the commitment level.

This range of levels of response often is the explanation for a problem that is common to many pastors with a strong orientation to social action. After several years of preaching with a heavy emphasis on the urgency of radical social change, he, or more often his successor, is bewildered when this congregation responds to a crisis with a tenacious grip on the status quo and vigorous opposition to change.

What may have happened was that the pastor thought he was receiving approval and an endorsement of his views from the congregation while most of the people in the pews were simply either receiving the message without any affirmative response or approving the concept of a free pulpit. Until the crisis, there had not been any request for the members to commit themselves either in support or in opposition of these views of their pastor. When that time did come, it turned out that the vast majority, who had been perceived as being either supportive or committed to the contents of the message, had only been acknowledging receipt of the message and possibly approving the preacher's right to voice his opinions.

The fourth basic assumption is that *two-way communication is far superior to one-way communication*. Despite the obvious merit of such a statement, most voluntary associations, including the churches, continue to function on the apparent assumption that one-way communication is adequate.

The widespread belief that one-way communication is adequate is illustrated by the methodology employed in tens of thousands of Sunday school classes, by the format used in countless conferences, training programs, and meetings, by the procedures used in developing and financing the programs of most local churches, and by the method of allocating quotas and apportionments for benevolences in many denominations.

The other side of this picture is that there is far more two-way communication in the churches than appears at first glance. Much of this two-way communication is in nonverbal terms. This includes the response of the person who is invited to a meeting but does not appear, the member who is deeply moved by the sermon but goes out a side door without even greeting the pastor after the Sunday morning service, the "failure" of many congregations to meet their assigned quota on benevolence giving, the visitor who is "church shopping" and never returns, and the $500 check in the special offering which was assumed might total $300 from all contributors.

It should also be added that an increasing number of congregations are deliberately and carefully structuring new opportunities for meeting full and effective two-way communication within the parish, and between the parish and the community. These include "talk-back" sessions after the Sunday morning worship service, encounter groups, "hearings" by the

139

regional denominational judicatory, open meetings of the governing body of the local church, visitations on all the members by listening teams in the parish, and systematic visits among non-members in the neighborhood of the church building. (See chapter 2 for an elaboration of how some local churches are building in better two-way communication.)

The last of the basic assumptions to be presented here is that *it is much easier to secure an adequate level of communication between two separate organizations than it is to secure an adequate level of communication within an organization.*

"We never have any misunderstandings or communication problems with the Presbyterian church down the street, but we sure have problems getting through to our own members," complained the rector of a 400-member Episcopal parish.

This Episcopal priest was describing a perfectly normal situation. The obstacles to achieving an adequate level of communication within a parish are far greater than in achieving an adequate level of communication between two parishes or between the parish and the diocese, conference, convention, or synod.

This means a much greater effort must be made in carrying on communication within the parish than in communicating with the church down the street. This means a greater degree of redundancy, the use of more different forms of intra-parish communication, more attention to developing two-way communication, and more emphasis on monitoring and evaluating the feedback.

While each one of these assumptions appears to represent the obvious, it is remarkable how often they are ignored in parish planning and how often faulty communication seriously inhibits the implementation process.

One of the methods for improving the quality of communication for reducing the number of needless misunderstandings, and for improving the quality of the decision-making process, is through the use of policy guidelines.

The Use of Policy Guidelines

"Why don't we adopt a permanent policy on the use of the fellowship hall? It seems to me we waste a lot of time at nearly every church council meeting discussing who can use the fellowship hall and who can grant permission for its use," complained a member at Mt. Pleasant Church.

"Before we call a pastor to replace the Rev. Mr. Johnson, we ought to adopt a policy on how much time the pastor should be granted for vacation, continuing education being a counselor at camp, and other denominational responsibilities that take him away from the parish," suggested a member of the pulpit committee at St. Peter's Church.

"Instead of spending one whole meeting on this every year, why don't we simply adopt a policy that every summer we will shift from two worship services to one, beginning with the second Sunday in June and ending with the first Sunday in September?" asked a member of the worship committee at Main Street Church.

Each of these three persons was suggesting that his church adopt a policy guideline that would provide a plan of action or a frame of reference or a decision in a certain set of circumstances.

There is no easier or better way to facilitate the

141

implementation process in the parish or in a denominational judicatory than by the adoption of a set of policy guidelines. There is no simpler method of avoiding unnecessary discussion and of conserving valuable committee time for more important questions than through the use of policies.

Among the most common policy statements encountered in local churches are those governing the use of the building, weddings, compensation and time off for ordained personnel, and bills that may be paid by the treasurer without first receiving approval of the governing body of the congregation. In recent years many congregations have begun to develop policies governing vacation, sick leave, and pension for lay employees; the delegation of responsibility to boards and committees; programs of in-service training for both lay leaders and clergy; rotation in office of leaders; and the priority system governing the preparation of the annual budget and the allocation of receipts.

The more complicated the problem and the more complex the organizational response to that problem, the more critical it is to have a series of carefully formulated policy guidelines. Policies are essential in any approach to a system as contrasted to the problem orientation which focuses on a single part or point of the larger system.

The central reason for adopting policy statements is simple. It is to guide the actions of people within the organization and to enable persons outside the organization to anticipate how that organization will respond in a given set of circumstances. It means that the response will be from the perspective of the entire organization rather than as a single response to what is often viewed as only an isolated problem.

Policies are guideline statements devised to assist decision-makers. The more advanced or the more sophisticated the organizational structure, the more likely it is that policy guidelines will have been prepared. In the newer, the more informal, the smaller, and the less sophisticated organization, the tendency is "to fly by the seat of the pants" in making decisions. As time passes, as traditions are established, and as the decision-making process becomes more complex, policy statements emerge.

Policy guidelines have several values for both the parish and for the denominational judicatory.

1. They are useful in translating general statements of purpose into terms that can guide the decision-making process.

2. They are useful in testing past and current practices and decisions against an official statement of purpose. Policy guidelines constitute one of the two or three best methods of offsetting the power of precedent in the budgeting process.

3. They tend to improve the quality of the planning and budgeting process.

4. They tend to produce consistent, coherent, and compatible decisions.

5. They expedite the decision-making process.

6. They offer a rationale for explaining decisions.

7. They tend to help keep the debate focused on the basic principle or policy behind a specific decision rather than on the details of a particular decision. This reduces the possibilities for diversionary controversy during debate from the floor.

8. They encourage long-range thinking and planning.

9. They permit the responsibility for many minor decisions to be delegated.

143

10. They tend to sharpen and keep in focus the purpose or function of the organization.

11. They reduce the chances of "boss-rule" in which one or two very knowledgeable leaders can "flood the floor debate" with a mass of detail that obscures the basic issues behind specific allocations of funds.

12. They provide an excellent basis for broadening the degree of participation in the decision-making process, for encouraging lay involvement, and for improving the quality of communication in "why" the church is involved in certain ventures.

Some churchmen may resist the idea of formulating and adopting policy guidelines. "It's too formal." "It sounds like you want to turn the church into a business." "They will get in the way of the Holy Spirit." "We're too small and too informal to need anything that fancy." These are some of the objections that often are heard when the subject is first introduced.

Comments such as these obscure the real issue. The question is not whether that parish will be guided by policy statements. The *decision-making process in every local church is guided by policy guidelines.* Usually they are referred to as customs, traditions, and precedents. The real question is whether these existing policies will be collected and utilized in a systematic manner or whether they will be followed in a highly informal fashion. In simple terms, what is involved here is the translation of customs, traditions, and precedents into more visible policies. Unless and until this translation and codification has been completed, the knowledgeable "old timer" in the parish has a tremendous psychological and tactical advantage over the layman who recently transferred his membership to that congregation and also over the new pastor. For some, this will be a valid reason for not formally adopting a set of policy guidelines.

The congregation or judicatory that develops and adopts a set of policy guidelines should realize that in addition to improving the quality of the decision-making process and facilitating the implementation of plans and programs, *it is also planting the seeds of blight, decay, decline, and irrelevance* unless it also builds in methods of keeping the guidelines from becoming too rigid. As in all aspects of the life of any social organization, there is always the pressure for the slave to become the master. The real choice, however, is not policies or no policies. The real choice is between using precedent, custom, and tradition as useful tools or letting them become the rulers.

Let's Vote on It

"All we ever do around here is talk, talk, talk! This time, instead of spending six months talking the subject to death, let's vote on it. That way we can find out how people feel and get this thing settled once and for all," argued one of the leading laymen in the Oak Grove Church, where they were discussing the possibility of a merger with Zion Church.

The comment of this impatient layman illustrates one of the most widely held myths in the implementation process in the local church. This is the belief that any controversial question can be disposed of by voting on it. In an amazingly large proportion of events, what were thought to be determinative votes when the ballots were cast subsequently turned out not to have been decisive.

145

In looking at the experiences of individual congregations, it is noteworthy that a great many of them first rejected by ballot a course of action that later was followed. This is illustrated by the congregations that first voted to remain at their old location and subsequently relocated, by the parishes that first rejected by secret ballot a proposed building program before going ahead with a new building, by the local churches that formally rejected the proposal to merge with a nearby congregation and later consummated that merger, and by the congregations that voted against allowing Negroes to join and later became biracial congregations. There is no law that requires one to be consistent and this also applies to local churches.

There is a valid generalization that says voluntary associations tend to reject any proposal for radical institutional change the first time it is introduced. This also applies to local churches. In other words, a local church often may have to vote no before it can say yes.

A second dimension of this question of what really is settled by a vote is illustrated by the proposed merger of the Oak Grove and Zion congregations. An affirmative vote by both congregations probably will settle the issue forever. A negative vote by one or both congregations may or may not settle that issue forever. Calling for a vote does not necessarily settle any question.

A third illusion in the voting process is that the votes are cast by a show of hands, a paper ballot, or by voice. Frequently such a formal vote is relatively meaningless. This can be seen in the annual meeting of the synod or conference or diocese when a motion to appropriate a sum of money is adopted, the

146

financial askings of the parishes are increased, but many of those voting affirmatively make no effort to increase the level of benevolence giving in their congregation when they return home. This is illustrated every week when the governing body of a local church unanimously approves a proposed new program in that parish, and then not one of the persons voting ever moves to help implement that program. The important votes in the implementation process often are cast with the feet or the hands or the pocketbook rather than with a yea or a piece of paper.

There are occasions when a formal vote is required in order to implement a program in the parish. When this happens, five caution signs should be observed.

First, do not ask people to vote prematurely. Allow time for them to become thoroughly acquainted with all facets of the issue. One of the pragmatic reasons for observing this warning is that whenever people are forced to vote prematurely, they tend to vote against change and the future and in favor of the status quo and the past.

Second, present only one issue at a time. "Should this congregation sell its property, unite with Zion Church, and together build a new structure on the Wright property?" To ask mere human beings to respond to such a complex question with a simple yes or no is unfair as well as unwise. Many organizations, including most governmental jurisdictions, require that each question on a ballot be listed separately. This is also a good rule for ecclesiastical organizations to follow. If, to use the Oak Grove–Zion example, it is necessary to have a vote on all four of the questions contained in this one proposition on the same day—and rarely is that really

147

necessary—they should be separated and voted on as four separate questions.

Closely related is a third caution. Whenever possible, avoid the use of a yes or no type of question in a ballot. When the alternatives of yes and no are the only ones presented, an affirmative vote usually produces a course of action that can be implemented. A negative vote usually is more difficult to interpret. Were those voting no against that particular proposal or were they voting in favor of the status quo.

A preferable procedure is to confront people with two affirmative choices, even if one is simply continuation of the status quo. "Do you favor this or do you favor that?" A question in a form similar to that usually will produce an affirmative sense of direction. Too often a congregation can be immobilized when it is found that maintaining the status quo is untenable, a new course of action is proposed, a yes or no ballot is prepared, and a majority vote against that proposal. What happens next?

While this statement is vulnerable to misinterpretation, a fourth word of caution is that in most voluntary organizations, including the local church, it often is unwise to let an issue come to a formal vote until most of the leaders are reasonably sure of the outcome of the balloting.

If no one can accurately predict the outcome of the voting, it probably means the vote is being held too soon. There has not been enough time for the necessary study, analysis, reflection, and discussion.

Furthermore, if the outcome is unpredictable, it may mean a very close vote. A voluntary association can act most effectively when moving from the base of a consensus, or at least with the support of a seventy- or eighty- or ninety-percent majority. A fifty-one-percent majority often is the same as a negative vote.

Perhaps most important of all, it is important to see a formal vote, not as the decisive point in the implementation process, but rather as the legitimatizing of a decision that already has been arrived at informally. If the decision already has been made informally, it should be possible to predict the outcome of the balloting.

Finally, an important consideration that should not be overlooked is the fact that education is alienating. Whenever a few people in a congregation share an educational experience that enlarges their vision, alters their definition of the purpose and mission of the church, or changes their system of values, this experience tends to alienate those few persons from the rest of the congregation.

A common example of this is in the congregation that is faced with a problem and a special committee is appointed to study it. The members of this special committee spend scores of hours studying the questions within the context of the purpose and mission of the church and unanimously recommend a specific course of action. This is submitted to a congregational vote and overwhelmingly defeated.

What happened? A normal, natural, and predictable sequence of events is represented by this example. The special committee had an educational experience that alienated them from the rest of the group, and the majority of the congregation rejected their proposal. A wiser course of action could have been developed by a careful analysis of the process of planned social change.

Planned Social Change

Why was this special committee's recommendation rejected? One reason may have been that they violated one or more of the basic principles in the process of planned social change.

In recent years, behavioral scientists have described the process of planned social change from within an organization. Before looking at this process, it should be emphasized that many of the changes that take place within organizations are the result of external pressures and forces. The Great Depression, an external force, radically changed the banking system in the 1930's. The decision by the Congress in 1956 to build an interstate highway network was an external force that radically changed hundreds of villages and cities. The Black Manifesto of 1969, again a force from the outside, radically changed the priority system in many denominations and congregations.

In looking at the process of planned social change from within an organization, however, it is possible to identify five important steps.

The first is *discontent*. Without discontent there obviously will be no change from within. The special committee mentioned in the previous section may have increased their own discontent with the status quo through careful study and analysis, but the majority of the congregation may not have shared this rising degree of discontent.

The effective change agent may find he has to spend considerable time and effort increasing the extent and intensity of discontent.

The second step in the process is the *formation of an initiating group* that will help turn the proposal into reality. Numbers here often become important and usually the larger and the more inclusive the supporting group, the more influential it will be and the greater the chances of success.

It is also important, and frequently crucial, to develop a supporting group that includes persons who can legitimatize or give a "stamp of approval" to the proposal, and who can supply the necessary resources of enthusiasm, skill, money, leadership, votes, expertise, and time that are required.

In this step, the original proposal, developed by the initiating group in step two, often is revised, amended, and frequently greatly improved in quality. As this happens, a larger number of persons identify the planned course of action as "mine."

This is the step in the process that often is skipped by those who identify a problem, develop a solution, and impatiently hurry on to the fourth step in the process. This may have been what defeated the special committee mentioned earlier.

This fourth step is *approval, execution, and implementation.* If it is an election, this is the vote. If it is a building program, this is construction. If it is a new ministry, this is the actual implementation of that ministry.

Frequently this step is anticlimactic if the necessary work has been completed during the first three steps.

The final step in this process of planned social change is *the institutionalization of the new proposal.* This is not always desirable or necessary. A proposal to have four congregations join in a union Thanksgiving service in November may follow the first four steps and omit the fifth if this is viewed as a one-time-only arrangement. The proposal to launch an intercongregational task force to oppose a specific bill in the state legislature probably should ignore this fifth step. On the other hand, one of the most common reasons for the high mortality rate among co-operative ministries is failure to institutionalize them.

This five-step process of planned social change is an important consideration that should be kept in mind by the person who is as concerned with the implementation of plans as he is with the generation of new ideas. Another subject that may be helpful is to review what appears to have made a difference in other parishes as they sought to implement new ideas.

What Makes a Difference?

What is the difference between the congregation with an outstanding record of ministry and service and the local church that appears to be having difficulty in responding effectively to the call of the Lord? What is the difference between the congregation that consistently is able to implement new ideas for ministry and the congregation that appears to be unable to get from the idea stage through the implementation process?

After a decade of working with 200 to 300 congregations a year, a dozen factors appear to stand out.

1. Do the members take the Bible seriously? Do they look at the Bible, not only as a record of God's concern for man and for his salvation, but also as a guidebook on the purpose and role of the church and as an accumulation of wisdom about the behavior of human beings and human institutions?

2. Is there an openness to the power of the Holy Spirit? Do the members believe, and act on the belief, that God is at work in his world today?

3. Is there a strong person-orientation in the life, program, ministry, and outreach of the congregation? Is the primary motivating force a desire to meet the needs of people, or is it on getting people to participate in "our program," or is the primary emphasis on maintaining the institution?

Is the primary emphasis on identifying and responding to the needs of people rather than on strengthening the institution? Perhaps the clearest illustration of this is found in the parish's approach to evangelism. In the person-centered parish the motivation is, "We need to share the good news of Jesus Christ with others." In the institution-centered parish, the motivation is "We need to get some more new members to help pay the bills and keep our church going."

This distinction can be seen throughout the life and program of the local church. Is the emphasis in the church school on increasing the attendance of the long-established Sunday school or on developing a program of Christian education that is relevant to the needs of contemporary man?

In the local church, as in private enterprise, it is becoming increasingly clear that one of the quickest ways to go out of existence is to concentrate on "doing business in the same way we have for years" rather than to focus on the needs of an ever-changing clientele.

4. Is the basic orientation toward the future? The congregation that is oriented toward today and tomorrow has a future. The congregation that is oriented toward yesterday may have a glorious past and an inspiring tradition, but it probably does not have a future.

A very simple test is to look at what happened at

153

the last anniversary celebration. It matters little whether this was the sixtieth anniversary of the founding of the parish, the fiftieth anniversary of the dedication of the building, or the tenth anniversary of the present pastor's coming to this congregation.

Was the dominant emphasis of the celebration on the past or on the future? Or, to go back to the third point above, was the focus on the building and the institution or on outreach and ministry to people?

5. Are there clearly defined, positive expectations about tomorrow?

One of the most influential forces in determining what will happen is the nature of the expectations about what will happen. In those parishes where there was the widely shared feeling "There just isn't much we can do anymore," little was accomplished. In those congregations where expectations were positive, goals were articulated, and carefully developed plans and schedules were formulated, the results often met or exceeded expectations.

In looking toward tomorrow, is the congregation projecting yesterday as tomorrow, or is it assuming that tomorrow will not simply be a repetition of yesterday?

6. Is corporate worship recognized as a central and crucial element in the life of the congregation? Is worship seen as a vital experience for the Christian or is it viewed as an obligation inherited from the past?

In an average month, what percentage of the total resident-confirmed membership attended at least one service of corporate worship? Twenty percent? Forty percent? Sixty percent? Eighty percent? The lower that percentage, the more doubtful the future of that parish.

Here again questions of orientation to the past or

the present, and of responding to the practices and traditions of the institution or to the needs of people should be raised. "This is the way we have always done it here and if that doesn't have meaning to you, well, perhaps you had better go elsewhere," is an attitude that may be presented in the interests of conserving cherished traditions, but too often it is received as a voice of rejection. Increasingly, the congregation that seeks to respond to the needs of people will have to diversify the opportunities for corporate worship.

Finally, a word should be added about the importance of preaching and the proclamation of the Word. While there is reason to believe that the demand for poor and mediocre preaching has dropped off sharply in recent years, the demand for excellent preaching probably never has been greater than it is today.

In congregation after congregation outstanding preaching has made an almost unbelievable difference in the life, vigor, and spirit of the parish. Dying parishes have been brought to life by good preaching. Congregations where the members have turned away from the community and concentrated on institutional maintenance have gained a new sense of mission and service from good preaching. Never underestimate the power of the Word!

7. Is the definition of purpose of the church clearly stated and widely understood? Does it unify or divide the membership? Or has the definition of the purpose, role, and mission of this parish never been articulated?

The most common cause of the polarization that has immobilized so many congregations today is a conflict over the definition of purpose. Does the

155

definition of purpose for this parish include evangelism? Social action? Community outreach? A concentration of resources on the care of members?

The lack of a definition of purpose tends to lead a parish to perpetuate yesterday's program, to reject innovation, and to drift about like a ship without a rudder.

8. Closely related are questions on trust and tolerance. Do the members trust one another? Do they trust the pastor? Does the pastor trust the members? Is there the depth of trust that enables people to work together despite differences on tactics or on priorities? Is there the tolerance of diversity that enables the various members to respond to differing calls to ministry and service? Is there the tolerance that recognizes and celebrates the manifold gifts of the Spirit that Paul described in the twelfth chapter of his first letter to the church at Corinth?

The greater the sense of mutual trust, the fewer the limitations on what a congregation can do. The greater the toleration of diversity, the larger the opportunities for ministry and for personal growth through study and response in service.

9. Is the base of participation and involvement growing? Is the proportion of members involved in making the decisions and carrying out the ministry of the parish larger this year than it was last year?

There is a tendency for this to become a self-perpetuating cycle, especially if the trend is toward more limited participation. As the participation base narrows, the natural tendency is to place the highest priority on institutional maintenance and continuing the traditional program. This leaves limited resources for other facets of ministry and reduces the opportunities for involving other people in those areas of service and ministry that utilize their special gifts and talents.

On the other hand, when a conscious and systematic effort is made to increase the proportion of members actively involved in setting policy, establishing priorities, making decisions, and carrying out the ministry of the parish, new opportunities are opened for the personal and spiritual growth of the individual as well as for expanding the ministry of that congregation.

The larger the congregation, the more urgent the need to systematically structure into the administration of the parish a method of assimilating newcomers, rotating leaders out of office and broadening the base of participation. It will not happen automatically!

10. Is there a recognition of the obligations the parish has to each member?

As a congregation begins to shrink in size and as it begins to decline in terms of institutional strength, there is a strong tendency to place an increasingly greater emphasis on what the members "owe" their church. "If only the people had a greater loyalty to their church" or "If people would remember the meaning of the vows they took when they were confirmed" are frequently heard comments.

More constructive and creative is the pattern that can be observed in the parishes that adapt to changing situations, that emphasize ministry rather than institutional maintenance, and that recognize and respond to the challenges of a new day.

While seldom articulated in this manner, in these parishes there is a recognition of a threefold obligation by the parish to the members.

The first part of this obligation consists of the

traditional ministry to members of corporate worship, education, fellowship, and pastoral care.

The second part includes a variety of opportunities for personal and spiritual growth—the nurture of the person. It has been pointed out elsewhere that the greatest return on the dollar investment in many congregations has been that budget item, typically one or two percent of the local budget, that is allocated to inservice training for laymen. Every local church has an obligation to provide its members with opportunities for personal and spiritual growth. The congregations that take this obligation seriously usually show signs of a new life. It is not difficult for an outsider to recognize the signs in the parish where members have participated in the Bethel Series of the Adult Christian Education Foundation or have attended the Ecumenical Institute or have been involved in some other serious lay training program.

Several congregations are combining a program of inservice training for laymen with a rotation plan for church leaders. One variation of this concept calls for the rotation of all elected parish leaders into a sabbatical year after three years of active service. During this sabbatical year, they may choose from a variety of training opportunities. Only those who participate in at least two training activities during their year out of office are eligible for nomination to leadership positions.

The third obligation of the local church to the members is to provide a variety of opportunities for the member to be involved in ministry and service to others. The recognition of this responsibility and the response of laymen may be the most exciting and significant trend in the parish today.

11. Is there a challenge to the members to commit

themselves to specific goals? Too many congregations appear to have dismissed the first and second chapters of the Epistle of James as heretical. When the members are challenged to be both believers and doers, when the idea that faith without works is a dead faith is presented, and when the members are asked to commit themselves to specific goals, it does make a difference! In too many congregations too little is asked of the members—and the response is in proportion to the challenge.

12. Has anything new been added to the program and ministry of the parish in the past year?

There is a tendency for the program of the long-established parish to resemble the attic where the old is preserved and nothing is ever discarded.

More impressive, however, are those parishes where each year one or two new elements are added to the total program and ministry as new needs are identified and responses are developed to these needs. Frequently this means one or two existing programs have to be terminated. Sometimes these are already nearly dead, sometimes they are obsolete but still very lively. In either case, a short-term view based on expediency may suggest continuing them, but the long-term view based on stewardship and relevance demands the reallocation of the resources that have been keeping obsolete old programs alive.

Here again the self-perpetuating cycle concept is appropriate. If the tradition is never to start anything new or to perpetuate the obsolete, it is very difficult to break that cycle. On the other hand, if the tradition is that every element in the life and ministry of the parish is evaluated periodically and those that are obsolete are replaced by new ministries, it is relatively easy to continue that cycle.

To go back to the central question raised at the beginning of this section, what makes a difference as churches seek to implement their plans?

It seems to make a difference if most or all of the questions asked here are answered affirmatively.

It also makes a difference if most or all of them are answered negatively!

Don't Scratch It!

"Why are you putting such a big bandage on his arm?" The mother of the nine-year-old boy was watching anxiously as the doctor spread a thin layer of ointment on his son's forearm and then covered it with a bandage from the wrist to the elbow.

"All he has is a very mild skin irritation and if he doesn't scratch it everything should be all right in three or four days," replied the doctor. "It does itch, however, and if he scratches it he can easily turn it into a major problem that will take months to cure. The bandage is to keep him from scratching it."

One of the most frequent unnecessary obstacles to ministry in the parish is the inclination of some persons to scratch minor irritations until they become inflamed and are major diversions in the life of that parish. It may be the way the minister has his hair cut, it may be the fact that the pledges in the every-member canvass totalled only 98 percent of the budget, it may be the youth group keeps cluttering up the fellowship hall, or it may be the way one of the ladies knits during church council meetings.

It is helpful to remember that very few baseball players bat a thousand for the season, very few marriages are flawless, and very few members of the local church are perfect.

160

There are hundreds of points of potential irritation in every marriage, in every family, and in every parish. If scratched often and hard enough, each one can become a major problem.

One of the ways to facilitate getting from here to there is to be able to recognize these as being only mild irritations and to resist scratching them.

SUGGESTIONS FOR FURTHER READING

Ackoff, Russell L. *A Concept of Corporate Planning.* New York: Wiley-Interscience, 1970.

Brower, Marvin. *The Will to Manage.* New York: McGraw-Hill, 1966.

Fisher, Wallace E. *Preaching and Parish Renewal.* Nashville: Abingdon Press, 1968.

Levitt, Theodore. *Innovation in Marketing.* New York: McGraw-Hill, 1962.

Moynihan, Daniel P. "Policy vs. Program in the '70's." *The Public Interest,* Summer 1970.

Nirenberg, Jesse S. *Getting Through to People.* Englewood Cliffs, N. J.: Prentice-Hall, 1963.

Odiorne, George. *Management Decisions by Objective.* Englewood Cliffs, N.J.: Prentice-Hall, 1969.

Schaller, Lyle E. *Planning for Protestantism in Urban America.* Nashville: Abingdon Press, 1965.

———. *The Local Church Looks to the Future.* Nashville: Abingdon Press, 1968.

Seifert, Harvey, and Clinebell, Howard J., Jr. *Personal Growth and Social Change.* Philadelphia: Westminster Press, 1969.

Sower, Christopher. *Community Involvement.* New York: The Free Press, 1958.

White, D. J. *Decision Theory.* Chicago: Aldine Publishing Co., 1969.

6

PLANNING FOR OUR TYPE CONGREGATION

"You simply cannot apply the usual generalizations about the church to our situation," commented the business administrator of a large downtown church in North Carolina. "Our situation is unique, there is no other church like ours, and you cannot even begin to talk about our problems and our future unless you recognize this!"

Was this man right or wrong in his analysis?

The answer is a clear-cut "yes!" He was right in that every parish is unique and that no congregation is exactly like any other congregation. (One person on hearing that statement remarked, "Yes, and let's be grateful for that. If every congregation were exactly like every other congregation, we could not find pastors for three fourths of them." A district superintendent, standing nearby, added "And if all pastors came out of the same mold and were identical, we couldn't place nine tenths of them!")

The church administrator was wrong, however, in that a few generalizations can be developed that apply to all congregations and many more can be developed that apply to certain types of local churches.

162

Since there are approximately one half million religious congregations in the United States today, it should be obvious there are very few generalizations that can be applied with equal validity and relevance to every one of these congregations. If, however, these congregations are grouped by categories, it is possible to develop generalizations that may be helpful to the leaders in the congregations that belong in the same category.

Before World War II, most of the 160,000 congregations in the twenty largest "mainline" Protestant denominations could be placed in one of three broad categories. The largest was the neighborhood church. This included tens of thousands of rural congregations all across the nation. It included the neighborhood churches in cities that had been organized to serve a specific geographical area. Many of these were organized during the first three decades of this century when the urban population of the United States jumped from 30 million in 1900 to 69 million thirty years later. Most of these new urban congregations were established to serve a relatively small geographical parish of perhaps two to six square miles.

The second category overlapped the first and included the tens of thousands of ethnic, racial, and nationality congregations. These included a German Methodist church in Rockford, Illinois, a Finnish Lutheran parish in Cleveland, a Negro congregation in rural Mississippi, a Dutch Reformed church in Holland, Michigan, a Romanian Baptist church in Chicago, a Japanese Methodist congregation in California, a German Lutheran parish in Wisconsin, and a Spanish speaking Presbyterian congregation in Texas. While many of these churches drew most or all of their members from a limited geographical area,

163

their dominant sociological characteristic was a language, ethnic, cultural, or racial tie.

The third, and smallest, general category was the downtown First Church. This congregation drew members from a comparatively large geographical area, the members usually came from the upper half of the socio-economic-educational strata of the community, and in nearly every city it was one of the most highly visible churches in the community.

These three broad general categories did not account for all the Protestant churches in the nation, but the vast majority could be placed in one of these three groups. The exceptions included the university church, the unique sect-type congregation, the institutional church in one of the larger cities, the cathedral-type parish that had a distinctive role in the regional judicatory of that denomination, and other categories. There were only a relatively few congregations in each of these specialized types, and together they accounted for less than a fifth of all congregations.

During the past three decades, however, the role and life of both individuals and institutions in American society has become more complex. One response to this increased complexity, and also one cause of an increasing complexity, has been an increase in specialization. Every effort to increase the sensitivity of the response to the needs of people as individuals and to groups of individuals has increased the degree of complexity and the extent of specialization. The churches have been a part of this trend. In recent years there has emerged within the churches a series of highly specialized vocations and ministries. The chaplain in a municipal hospital, the pastor to the jazz community in Greenwich Village, the community organizer in Chicago, the minister of music in a local church, the executive of a council of churches, the denominational staff person responsible for leadership training, the campus minister, the parish worker in a local church, and the professional church business administrator represent only a few of the jobs in this growing list of specialized ministries.

Before going on to identify a few of the types of congregations that cover the ecclesiastical landscape today, it may be helpful to review four trends that have affected the definition of these categories.

The most highly visible is the disappearance of the nationality or language parish and denomination. This can be seen most clearly in Roman Catholicism, where literally hundreds of what formerly were nationality parishes (German, Slovene, Czech, Italian, Polish, Croatian, Hungarian, Slovak, etc.) have either become geographical parishes or have merged with geographical parishes. (One Catholic observer described this transition with the comment, "They all became Irish Catholic parishes.") The same pattern can be seen in American Protestantism. The typical pattern has been to begin using the English language in corporate worship with this step followed, usually a few decades later, by the dropping of any distinctive nationality image. For example, most German Methodist congregations were using English for worship by the end of the first World War, but it was over two decades later before the German Methodist Annual Conferences had been absorbed into the geographical conferences. Several of the nationality Lutheran denominations began using English in the first third of this century, but they continued as distinctive entities until the mergers that produced the Lutheran Church in America and the American Lutheran Church in the early 1960's.

As is true with most generalizations, however, the change in the number of nationality and language congregations has not been entirely in one direction. One result of the immigration of 6 million persons into the United States between 1945 and 1970 was the creation of hundreds of new Latvian, German, Greek, Italian, Hungarian, Puerto Rican, Portuguese, Japanese, and Indian congregations.

The most significant of these four trends has been the gradual disappearance of the geographical parish, especially in urban communities. A generous estimate would be that today perhaps five percent of the Protestant congregations in urban America can be described as basically or primarily geographical parishes. In the other ninety-five percent, three or four or five considerations are more significant than the place of residence of the members in describing the characteristics of that congregation.

Perhaps the least noticed of these four trends has been the gradual disappearance of the three-generation congregation. Again, this has been most common in Caucasian urban areas where it has coincided with the disappearance of the three-generation family and the elimination of the three-generation neighborhood. Today, relatively few white grandchildren are in the same congregation with their white grandparents. Hundreds of Negro congregations in urban and rural America constitute a major exception to this generalization.

The fourth of these trends is the gradual recognition of the importance of place in the lives of people. During the past two decades, sociologists, social psychologists, and other behavioral scientists have discovered that people naturally seek out familiar places. When they are forced out of familiar places this tends to produce emotional and mental tension. This is most apparent among older persons. Herbert Gans and Marc Fried reported this from their studies of the impact on persons forced to move by urban renewal projects. The same point has been documented in studies of older persons moving into housing projects for the elderly, in studies of friendship patterns among college students and "neighboring" patterns among young couples moving into their first home. There is a lesson in this for those who casually suggest "that church should be closed and all of the members should join this church over here."

Today, even an elementary listing of the categories of church types would include the metropolitan church (there are perhaps 400 to 500 of these in the United States, with a combined confirmed membership of over one million persons), the downtown "First Church" type congregation, the neighborhood church in the central city or the older suburb (with subcategories under this grouping), the nationality or language congregation, the black church (again with several subcategories), the "gathered congregation" that is trying to perpetuate yesterday, the specialized urban congregation, such as the university church, the intentional nongeographical urban parish, the "Memorial" church dominated for decades by one person or one family, the new suburban mission, the church in a racially changing community, the long-established congregation on the rural-urban fringe, the fifteen- or twenty-year-old suburban congregation, the "First Church" in the county seat town, the small, open-country congregation, the

167

church in the small trading center, and the church in the dying crossroads village. One of the most significant new types of emerging parishes, as Christians seek to respond with greater sensitivity to an increasingly complex society, is the congregation that deliberately seeks to be an agent of reconciliation in a world where society has become increasingly fragmented and polarized. This is not an exhaustive listing of types; some congregations will not fit into any one of these categories, and the categories are not completely mutually exclusive.

It also is possible to cut the cake in another direction and to define such categories as the growing congregation, the family church, the dying church, the subsidized church, the church in mission, and the churches which are emerging today to reach and minister to certain distinctive life styles in society.

Why Bother?

The value of these categories is not in their neatness, for they are not neat, discrete categories, but in their usefulness in local church administration and parish planning. Church leaders, like architects and planners, tend to act on preconceptions rather than from a reality base. The use of these categories may help to encourage the making of decisions based on reality rather than on preconceptions.

The use of these categories can be very helpful to a pulpit committee as they search for a new minister and to a clergyman as he tries to define his role. As a pastor moves from a parish of one type to a congregation of a different type, it is helpful if he realizes that he not only is changing churches, *but he also is moving from a church of one type to a church of a differ-*

ent type. Many of the problems encountered by pastors result from a neglect of this fact.

The mayor of a small town in Georgia carries the same job title as the mayor of Detroit, but it is entirely different job! Similarly, the minister of a fifteen-year-old, 800-member, suburban congregation, who becomes the pastor of a 1,000-member, downtown church, may be called "Pastor" in both parishes, but he not only has changed jobs, he also has exchanged job descriptions. After a couple of years in the downtown church, he may say to a friend, "The demands on the ministry certainly have changed in the past few years!" A more accurate statement might be, "When I moved from my former parish to this congregation, I not only changed congregations, I also changed roles, and I am just beginning to realize what a tremendous change that was!" Closely related to this is the value of this concept to persons engaged in a multiple staff ministry. The role of each person and the relationships among these persons are affected by the type of church they are serving. To be a church business administrator in a metropolitan type congregation is a different responsibility than to hold the same title in an 1,800-member suburban congregation. The relationship of the associate minister to the pastor in a 1,200-member county seat congregation in Iowa is different from the relationship of the associate minister to the pastor in old First Church in downtown Miami.

The use of these categories also can be very helpful as people in a congregation look to other congregations for ideas, models, and cooperative ministries. The large downtown Presbyterian Church in Rockford probably has more in common with the Lutheran, Episcopal, United Methodist, and United

Church of Christ congregations in the central business district of Rockford than with the other Presbyterian congregations in the presbytery. Likewise, the members of the open-country Presbyterian church in southern Indiana probably can learn more from talking with members of similar type United Methodist, Disciples of Christ, Brethren, Baptist, Church of God, and United Church of Christ congregations than with an equal number of people from other congregations in the Presbytery.

This point also is illustrated by many books that have appeared in recent years. *From Tradition to Mission* by Wallace Fisher is an excellent book for use by leaders in the old downtown congregation, while *Christ's Suburban Body* by Bailey and McElvaney, and Shippey's *Protestantism in Suburban Life* are directed at persons in the relatively new suburban congregation.

The members of a parish that is changing from one type to a different type also may find that this concept offers a useful frame of reference. Everyone naturally turns to look to the past for guidance. This is normal and natural, since a person knows the past with greater certainty than he knows the future. There are obvious values and benefits in turning to past experiences for guidance. There is great danger in this, however, for the local church that is changing from one type of congregation to becoming a different type of parish.

A sixty-year-old farmer, who had been a member for over four decades of what is now a fifty-five-member congregation forty miles west of Chicago, was asked what he saw in the future for his church. He described how the farms in that part of the county were being purchased by real estate developers and mentioned that over seven hundred new homes had been built in that school district in the past year. He concluded his observations by saying, "I don't see much future for this church unless some farmers start moving back in, and I don't think they will with farmland around here selling at over $4,000 an acre."

He was right! That local church does not have a future as a rural-farm congregation. It has a future only if it changes from that type of congregation to a type that is compatible with the suburbanization of that county.

The opportunities open to a local church and the demands on a congregation vary among different types of churches. As a congregation changes from one type to a different type, these opportunites and demands also change. This change from one type or category to a different type tends to occur over a period of several years. The perception of this shift by the membership tends to lag behind the acutal events. Furthermore, some members perceive this change and become aware of the implications much sooner than do others. This change, this lag in perceiving what is happening, and the differences among the members in the rate of recognition of these changes often can be a major source of dissension, tension, and conflict within a congregation.

Perhaps the most helpful way to illustrate the value of looking at local churches by type would be to describe the characteristics, opportunities, and style of ministry of churches in each category, to add some generalizations about the questions and problems facing congregations of each type, and to suggest criteria that can be used in a self-evaluation process. That is not possible in a book of this nature. It simply is not economically feasible to allocate three hundred pages to one chapter. It is possible, however, to discuss briefly from four different perspectives, and by using four different approaches, each of four types of parishes. These have been selected to represent four types that have unusually pressing problems as the members begin to plan for tomorrow. Hopefully, these comments will be useful to readers concerned with one of these four types, and will suggest to others how this concept can be applied in congregations of other types.

A Reappraisal at Old First Church

The two types of Protestant congregations facing the most tension-producing problems in the 1970's are the small rural church with 25 or 40 or 75 members and "Old First Church."

Thousands of the former and dozens of the latter types have disappeared from the scene during the past two decades. More will either adapt to changing conditions or become extinct during the 1970's.

During the first dozen years following the close of World War II, the most common admonition heard by leaders at Old First Church as they discussed their church's ministry, program, and future was, "Develop and maintain a program of excellent music, great preaching, and outstanding Christian education." This was good advice for the 1940's and the 1950's. It no longer is as useful as it was five, ten, or fifteen years ago.

Why? Why is a reappraisal necessary when the old formula worked so well for so long? Has the holy trinity of preaching, music, and Sunday school lost its power? If so, why?

172

There are many explanations and not all of them apply to every congregation; but a half dozen appear with remarkable frequency.

1. The number of restless Christians is growing. An increasing number of laymen have been listening to some of those great sermons, they have been reading those books that describe the church as mission, and they have been attending those conferences where the participants are urged to act out their Christian convictions. A significant number of the members at Old First Church have been believing what they have been hearing and reading. It is very disruptive when people begin to take the gospel seriously. It is even more disruptive when laymen take the gospel seriously but their local church does not appear to do likewise.

2. The competition is tougher. Other congregations have been constructing better church buildings (in American society the new often appears to be more attractive to some people than the old, especially if it is paid for), other churches have programs in Christian education that equal or excel that at Old First Church, television has reduced the comparative attractiveness of some types of preaching and perhaps most significantly of all, scores of competing organizations, movements, and opportunities have emerged through which the committed layman can express his convictions.

3. There is a rebellion against size and depersonalization. There is growing demand for involvement, participation, and self-determination.

The three most highly visible examples of this trend on the world scene are nationalism, the civil rights movements, and the revolt of the youth.

In the family and in the local church this trend

173

can be seen in the attitudes and actions of women and youth.

One result is that the large congregation which specialized in excellence rather than involvement, which had a relatively narrow definition of program, and which provided programs *for* people is no longer as attractive to many persons as the smaller congregation which emphasizes participation, involvement, diversity, and an acceptance of differences.

4. The democratization of the decision-making process has created new patterns of ministry. During the first half of this century it was not uncommon to find congregations dominated by one person or by one or two or three families. This was most common in small-town and rural churches, in Old First Church, and in Lutheran congregations. Sometimes this dominant authority figure was the pastor, sometimes it was a layman.

The climate of the last half of this century calls for a much broader base of authority. This change has occurred or is occurring in most congregations—and many of the congregations in which it did not occur have dissolved, merged, or relocated. The new pattern is most common in new missions organized since 1960.

There are still many First Churches, however, which are dominated by one or two leaders who plan for the congregation and who decide what is good for that church. A common result is either a re-evaluation of purpose and program, or a diminution in interest, participation, membership, and giving.

5. Changes in American society and in the functions of the central city have altered the role and changed the opportunities open to Old First Church. Yesterday a downtown location was an asset

simply in terms of the system of public transportation. Today the condition of public transportation systems makes a downtown location a liability in hundreds of cities, especially on Sunday or in the evening. To a limited degree, this decline of public transportation has been offset by the freeway system which brings many more people within fifteen-minutes driving time.

Yesterday the central business district was the place where "the action is." Today the action has moved out to suburban shopping centers and to recreation and entertainment facilities on the outskirts of the city. Today one of the quietest places in the city at night is (may be) the central business district.

Yesterday apartment construction tended to be concentrated in and around the central business district. Today the vast majority of new apartments being constructed are far from the central business district.

Yesterday the downtown church had an "automatic clientele" composed of spinsters and widows. In the 1950's, these two categories constituted thirty to forty percent of the membership of many downtown congregations. Today the spinster is disappearing from the population. In 1940, nineteen percent of all women age 35–44 had never married. By 1970, that figure had dropped to thirteen percent and it is continuing to decline. Today the traditional poor widow is being replaced by a rapidly growing new population group. This group is composed of comparatively well-to-do widows in the over-fifty age bracket. The combination of social security, private pension funds, widespread home ownership, hard working and thrifty husbands who died "prematurely," life insurance, and medical discoveries that

175

have prolonged the life expectancy of mature women is producing millions of widows who can live where they wish.

Yesterday, when the structure that houses Old First Church was constructed, it was customary to design libraries, banks, courthouses, city halls, and churches in a style that resembled a fortress. Today, instead of designing such buildings in a manner that tends to repel people, it has become the fashion to design these structures so they will be inviting and attract people. One result is that scores of these congregations are housed in buildings that are structurally sound, but are functionally obsolete and esthetically repulsive.

Yesterday the central business district was the place where nearly every prominent business and community leader spent his working day. The downtown church had an obvious distinctive appeal to these men. It also was easy to be in contact with them during the day. Today the changing economic function of the central city means that in over a hundred central cities only a small proportion of businessmen and community leaders spend their working days in the central business district. Today many outlying churches have a better location for ministering to these men during the week, especially if they have an adequate parking lot!

Yesterday the central business district was a relatively safe place. Today the people are frightened by a rising crime rate in the central city. In 1969, the number of robberies per 1,000 residents in the large central cities was nearly ten times the rate in the suburbs and nearly forty times the rate in rural areas. The chances of being assaulted, raped, or murdered were three times greater in the large central cities than

176

in the suburbs. Today the expansion of the inner-city slum area, the increase in crime, and especially the *fear* of crime and violence, has drastically changed the options open to Old First Church. In some cities this has already occurred and completely eliminated all of the traditional program except for Sunday morning. In a score of cities it has even eliminated most congregations of this type. In a couple of hundred American cities the reaction to the rising fear of crime and violence is now in progress. In another hundred urban communities no one yet comprehends the point of this paragraph. During the 1960's, the rate of increase in the number of violent crimes was ten times the rate of the population increase. As this continues, more congregations will recognize this to be a major factor in their planning.

A common result of this increase in crime and the fear of violence is that the insurance premiums at Old First Church have doubled or tripled and annual expenditures for maintenance (the repair of damage by vandals) has quadrupled. The funds that might have been allocated to program now are being used for the protection of persons and property.

6. Major changes are occurring in Christian education. The church, and especially the downtown First Church, that still regards Christian education as synonymous with Sunday school will have increasing difficulty in reaching people. Today a good Christian education program includes a range of emphases. In one class the emphasis—and attraction—may be on the content, in another it may be the supportive fellowship of the group, in a third it may be personal and spiritual growth, in a fourth it may be on functional competence, and in a fifth it may be training in articulating the faith. In many

177

congregations one half or two thirds of these classes may meet at a time other than Sunday morning.

This shift from the traditional emphasis at Old First Church in preaching, music, and Sunday school reflects one set of changing circumstances.

Before moving to another subject, however, a point that was mentioned in an earlier chapter merits the emphasis of repetition. The experiences of downtown churches today demonstrate very clearly that there is still a great demand for excellent preaching. The demand for poor or average preaching may be dropping rapidly, but the demand for outstanding preaching never has been greater. The supply may be diminishing, however.

In looking to the future of this type congregation, three additional points deserve mention here. First is the decentralization trend, which has only begun to be felt in some cities in the 25,000 to 150,000 population range, but which will continue to develop. As it does, there will emerge more new congregations that will be competitive with the First Churches. Old First Church will find it more difficult to attract people from the newly developing outlying areas.

Second is the importance of a distinctive purpose and identity. What is the distinctive purpose of the congregation? What is its role? What are the objectives? What are its unique characteristics? Increasingly it is important for Old First Church to develop a distinctive style which helps people see clearly its purpose, role, and goals.

Third, as each of these congregations seeks to accomplish its purpose and fulfill its ministry, what are the criteria by which it will determine the direction it is going and measure the rate of progress?

178

What indicators will be checked periodically to determine what is happening?

While it is impossible to provide a list of criteria that will be ideal for every First Church, there are several that often are helpful.

1. Does the number of persons received into membership by confirmation or profession of faith exceed the number of deaths?

2. What is the ratio of persons joining First Church by transfer (letter) compared to those leaving by transfer? This is a single and fairly reliable index of how "church shoppers" and newcomers view First Church. In most years, transfers in should exceed transfers out.

3. What is the attendance at worship to membership ratio? In large (over 1,000 members) First Churches this seldom exceeds fifty percent, but when it drops down to twenty-five to thirty percent, it may be a sign of trouble.

4. How many weddings were celebrated in First Church last year? How many in which *both* the bride and the groom were non-members? How many in which one or both of the marriage partners were members, but their parents were not members? Do the answers to these three questions say something to the way young adults see First Church?

5. What do recent new members say when asked, "Why did you join *this* congregation?" Among the strong downtown First Churches of today an increasing proportion of new members are giving answers such as these. "I joined because I was impressed by what this church is doing in this city." "Good preaching." "This church challenged me to carry out my ministry." "There is something going on here." "It's

179

alive!" "The fellowship opportunities." "It's the only church in town interested in young adults."

6. How well are new members assimilated into the life, fellowship and *leadership* of the congregation? Is the turnover in the leadership as great as the turnover in the membership?

7. What is the giving level? What is the trend in giving? Annual receipts from members in large First Churches with a multiple staff tend to average between $200 and $400 times the average attendance at worship, and should be closer to $300 than to $200.

8. What is the level of clerical and secretarial salaries? While this may sound very unimportant to some members, it is worth noting that in several dying and irrelevant downtown churches the salaries of the lay employees have been twenty to forty percent below the market level for comparable positions. The downtown church that is looking forward to yesterday often pays its employees on yesterday's salary scale.

9. How diversified is the program? The program at First Church should be varied in content and should provide a variety of opportunities for members to carry out their own ministry.

The other side of this issue is reflected in the inclination of some members and some downtown congregations to define the purpose and ministry of their church in very narrow terms. A common example is the pastor or layman who declares, "This is what I hear the Lord calling us to do and this is how we should respond to that call. If you don't hear the same call I hear and see the same avenue of response that I see, obviously you are not a Christian!" While the phrasing has been exaggerated, the thoughts behind the words are commonplace. This condition is sometimes described as the First Commandment problem.

The First Commandment problem is a real barrier to ministry and mission in many congregations, but is especially troublesome in Old First Church type parishes. The answer to the problem can be found in Romans 12:3-21 and I Corinthians 12:4-31.

10. When was a new element of ministry, a new program, or a new opportunity for service added to the total ministry of this congregation? Does it "shut down" in the summer? Or is the summer seen as an opportunity for new experiments in programming? A disproportionately large number of people who move to the city arrive in the summer. What is this congregation saying to them?

11. What proportion of the total receipts are spent on maintaining a meeting place and other forms of institutional maintenance? What percentage for outreach? For evangelism? For witness and service? Are these proportions changing?

12. What is the role of First Church in the ecumenical scene? Typically, First Church is one of the most active participants in the local ecumenical picture. When this is true, it is important, however, to ask, "Is this involvement in ecumenicity a means of ministry or a substitute for ministry?"

A New Agenda for the Small Rural Church

There are at least 200,000 rural congregations scattered across the continental United States. Many of these meet for worship in buildings out in the open country. Some meet in private homes, schools, town halls, vacant stores, and other buildings. A substantial number meet in well-maintained church buildings in mall towns and crossroads communities.

In many of these communities, the church is the last of the many institutions that once served that community. The blacksmith's shop was put out of business by the tractor, the automobile and the paved road forced the retail stores and the bank to close, and consolidation closed the doors of the public school.

At least three fourths of these congregations have fewer than one hundred members and a majority have fewer than sixty active, resident, confirmed members.

In discussing the future of these small churches one frequently hears two points of view.

The first is shared by a majority of the members of these small congregations. In this point of view the emphasis is on keeping the church open and on what may simply be described as survival goals. How can we be sure to have a preacher? How can we meet our financial obligations? These questions tend to recur when people sharing this view talk about the future of their church.

The second point of view is articulated by a minority of the members of these small congregations, by many pastors and laymen from larger congregations, and by a few denominational leaders.

Here the emphasis is on economy and efficiency. The small rural congregation with forty or eighty members is regarded as an inefficient and expensive operation with a limited ministry, an unfortunate orientation to the past and a limited view of the future. In terms of modern transportation or the consolidation of the public schools or contemporary shopping habits, these small rural congregations appear to be obsolete expressions of the church.

From this point of view the obvious course of action is to encourage two or three or four or five of these small churches to merge and form one congregation that is large enough to be a viable unit in terms of membership, leadership, program, and financial resources. In other cases the small rural church is encouraged to consider merger with the 400-member city congregation eight miles away. If people from that rural neighborhood can go in to town to shop, to attend high school and for entertainment, why can't they drive eight miles to go to church? After all, it takes many city people fifteen minutes to drive from their home to church; why are these rural folks so determined to hang on to their church?

What happens when people representing these two points of view meet to discuss the future of the small rural congregation?

More often than not everyone goes home frustrated. Those holding the first point of view wonder why "they" are so determined to close "our" church. Can't they understand what this church means to us, our parents, and our neighbors? Can't they see that for many of our older members, and most of our members have passed their fiftieth birthday, this building is a sacred place? Can't they see the people here are profoundly unhappy by the threat of losing this place on which so much of their sense of self-identity rests? Can't they understand there is a vast difference between a fifteen-year-old boy going into town to high school and asking that boy's sixty-five-year-old grandmother to give up her church and go into town to worship? If our church closed where would these children go to Sunday school? If our

183

church is closed half the members simply will stop attending worship anywhere. Why can't people see that?

Representatives of the second point of view go home wondering why the members of this small rural church are so stubborn. Why can't they comprehend the advantages of being a part of a larger congregation? Why can't they see that by merging they could offer a better Christian education for their children? Why can't they see that merger also would create more opportunities for a variety of involvement in the life and ministry of the church for both the adults and the young people? In addition to all of these advantages in program and ministry, the larger congregation could offer a more effective witness to Christ in the community. They could allocate a much smaller proportion of the church budget to maintaining the building and paying a preacher and put more into program and missions. Obviously all of the logical arguments are on the side of consolidation.

Is there any way to break this deadlock? Can people holding these contrasting points of view ever engage in meaningful dialogue? Can this communications barrier be broken?

One answer to these questions is to develop a new agenda for such meetings. The development of this new agenda requires three related changes.

The first required change is in the perspective of the participants. Instead of focusing on institutions, as both of the groups mentioned earlier were doing, it is far more helpful to direct attention to the mission and ministry of the church. Instead of talking about the means of ministry, it may be more fruitful to discuss purpose and performance. Instead of emphasizing survival, it usually is more constructive to talk about service. Instead of viewing the small rural church as a "problem" that needs to be "solved" or "eliminated," it is much more creative to view these congregations as "opportunities" for reaching people with the gospel.

Another requirement is for all participants to agree on a common objective. What is the purpose of this meeting? Why did we come together tonight? A very helpful response to these questions is the strengthening, reinforcing, and expansion of the ministry of the church. If this, rather than the maintenance of institutions, can be the objective of all the people involved in the discussion, the results are likely to be far more creative.

Traditionally the members of the small rural church have been confronted with three or four alternatives. (1) As long as you can pay your bills and as long as you can get a preacher, you can keep going on as you have in the past. (2) You can unite with one or two or three other small congregations to form one larger congregation. (3) Perhaps you can merge with the church in town. (4) You can dissolve this congregation and the members can find new church homes.

It is difficult to describe such a list as either inspired or inspiring. To many people in the small rural church the presentation of such a list can be boiled down to one thought, "They're determined to close our church!" It must be acknowledged, however, that for some small rural churches today this is the complete list. For many more congregations the list of alternatives is much longer.

The actual experiences of many small rural congregations reveal five other alternatives that may be added to that list. The first two are available to nearly every small congregation *if the members are open to new ideas,* while the last three depend on the cooperation of other congregations.

The most exciting of these alternatives requires a redefinition of the role of the laity. Too often the layman defines his role as being ministered to by the church, and especially by the pastor, and helping to "support" the church. This support of the church usually is limited to contributions of money to the church and of time to management of the institution.

When the role of the laity is defined in broader terms of "ministry," a long list of challenging possibilities is opened up as what used to be called "problems" are now seen as "opportunities." This can be illustrated by looking at three complaints heard frequently in the small church.

The first is, "We share a minister with two other congregations and this means we have to cut our worship service to forty-five minutes, we have to schedule the time to suit the convenience of the other churches, and the preacher arrives about ten seconds before the service is to begin and leaves about one minute after pronouncing the benediction."

Another common complaint is, "Our minister has to have a full-time job in order to make a living, that means there is little calling in the homes of members and almost no calling on the unchurched families." Sometimes this is expressed in these words, "Our minister is in school all week and I was in the hospital and out again before he even knew I was sick."

The third complaint goes something like this, "Our church is small and we can't pay a very big salary. As a result, whenever we get a good minister, he gets a call to a larger congregation just about the time he has become acquainted with the people and the needs in this community. It seems we spend a third of the time waiting for the man we have called to arrive, a third of the time getting acquainted with him, and a third of the time looking for a replacement after he accepts a larger church."

In these illustrations the minister is identified as the person who leads corporate worship, who ministers to the members, who serves as the evangelist for the congregation, who is the source of new ideas for ministry, and who is the symbol of the church in the community.

In those congregations where the role of the layman has been redefined in broader terms, these complaints are identified as opportunities for ministry, for service, and for personal growth for members of the congregation. In these congregations laymen frequently lead the Sunday morning worship service, laymen call on the members and the sick, laymen identify needs and initiate plans for new ministries, and laymen stand out as the symbol of the church in that community.

In one such parish, composed of eight rural congregations and served by one full-time ordained minister with a student assistant, there is a worship service in every church every Sunday at a time that is set by members of that congregation. A corps of nineteen lay preachers has been trained to lead corporate worship. On a typical Sunday the pastor and his assistant each will preach in one or two of the churches and the other four or five pulpits are filled by trained laymen who are paid for this service.

Other members are trained to call on members in their homes, to visit the hospitalized, and to call on the unchurched.

187

The most obvious advantage of this alternative is that it solves the "peak hour" problem on Sunday morning by providing additional trained leadership for the worship service.

This, however, is only one of several benefits in this approach. In addition it offers the opportunity for laymen to articulate and deepen their faith. One of these lay preachers emphasized this point with the statement, "You really can't begin to understand the gospel until you are called on to tell others about Jesus Christ."

In church after church this approach to ministry has changed the basic attitude of the membership from one of pessimism to optimism; it has raised the level of expectations of the members for themselves and their church; it has broken the dependency on the preacher that had limited the people's view; it has set laymen to theologizing about their daily lives and work; it has renewed the spirit of the participants; it has encouraged laymen to demand opportunities for training in ministry; and it has opened the door to other new approaches to innovation.

At one synod meeting where this alternative was being discussed, one person asked, "If laymen are going to do all of the preaching and calling, what will the minister do? Sit home and read?"

This brings up a second alternative open to the small rural church as it looks to the future—a redefinition of the role of the minister.

In American Protestantism one of the major goals of most small congregations has been to have its own full-time pastor. The church that shares a minister with another congregation and the church that is served by a minister with a secular job both look forward hopefully to the day when "we can have our

own minister." In large part this is based on a definition of the role of the pastor as a "doer." He does
the things that must be done—preaching, administration, counseling, calling, planning, evangelism, and
some teaching.

In some congregations, however, the Presbyterian
definition of the minister as the "teaching elder" is
taken seriously. In these congregations the primary
role of the minister is not as a doer, but as a teacher,
an enabler and trainer. His role resembles that of the
football coach who is training others to develop their
full potential. Like the effective coach, he must have
a good relationship with the players or he cannot
help them develop their talents. No one expects the
coach to carry the ball. Occasionally a team has a
player-coach, but most good coaches are far more
interested in training others to play than in playing
themselves. A few may send in the signals for every
play, but this usually reflects a defect in the coach's
confidence rather than in the ability of the players.

Every person who comes out for the team, even
in the schools which operate with a "no-cut" policy,
soon realizes that a sense of discipline is an essential
element in the successful team. The person who gives
less than his best may be permitted to dress for the
game and to sit on the bench, but if he expects to
play he knows this means continued effort at self-
improvement. Every coach realizes he must always
be seeking and training new talent.

Some clergymen can adapt to this new role very
easily, others cannot. This requires a radical shift in
the perspective of the members and of how they see
the role of the pastor.

Unlike the traditional alternatives of merger and
dissolution, these two alternatives—redefining the

role of the laymen and that of the pastor—stress change by addition rather than by subtraction.

Three other alternatives that merit consideration of the small rural church require cooperation with other congregations.

The first, and the most common, is sharing a pastor with another congregation. Sometimes this is with a congregation of another denomination. Thus, a Presbyterian congregation may share a pastor with a United Methodist Church or a United Church of Christ congregation. This is usually referred to as a "yoked field." More often, however, one pastor is shared by two or three congregations of the same denomination.

An important refinement of this concept is where the larger congregation in town shares a pastor with one or two open country or village churches. In this arrangement this minister serves as the associate pastor in the church in town on a part-time basis and also is the part-time pastor of one or two small congregations. Usually this arrangement is strengthened if the senior minister in the church in town occasionally preaches in the rural churches and the associate preaches occasionally in the church in town. Thus, the members of each congregation identify both ministers as "pastors."

A second alternative is to redefine the functions of the church. Traditionally the functions of the congregation have been defined in "either-or" terms. Either the congregation is large and strong enough to offer a certain program or ministry or that is denied the members. For example, if the church is not large enough to have a membership training class, new members do not have the benefit of this experience.

Today this concept is being challenged by many

small congregations. Usually the small church carries
out certain responsibilities by itself such as Sunday
morning worship, Sunday school, ownership and care
of a meeting place, its own benevolence program, and
has its own governing board.

Several other ministries are carried out cooperative-
ly with other congregations. This list may include the
daily vacation Bible school, the youth fellowship,
teacher training programs, special study groups for
young adults, work camps for high school youngsters, various forms of witness in the community, a
ministry to non-members, a ministry on issues, and
even in some cases the Women's Auxiliary.

Another alternative that merits consideration is a
more structured form of intercongregational cooperation in which several congregations constitute one
parish with its own professional staff. This may be
three congregations and one full-time minister or it
may include ten to fifteen congregations with three to
five professional staff members.

This "larger parish" is far from a new concept, but
it has been improved in recent years as a result of the
lessons learned from experience. Four of these lessons
merit mention here. First, it is advisable to build in
strong lay leadership from the very beginning. Second, each congregation should remain as a separate
organization with responsibility for the care and maintenance of its own meeting place. Third, if it is developed as a means for saving money it probably will
not function effectively for more than a year or two.
Fourth, when the care and maintenance of the parish
becomes an end in itself it is time to dissolve the
arrangement.

When adopted as a means of strengthening and

191

expanding the ministry of the churches, as a means for opening up new opportunities for ministry by the laity, and as a means of reaching more people with the gospel, it has tremendous possibilities.

As these small rural churches look toward tomorrow and as the members wonder what tomorrow will bring, they can begin their planning process with a simple five-question agenda.

1. The most obvious, and often the most pressing, is the rising cost of pastoral leadership. Today literally thousands of small rural churches are paying $.60 to $1.25 per member per week for the financial support of a pastor. This compares to $.25 to $.75 per member per week in the large city churches.

For most small rural churches this figure has doubled or tripled during the past twenty-five years, and probably will rise to approximately $2.00 per member per week by 1980.

Are the members of this small rural church willing to pay this price for pastoral leadership?

2. Relatively few small rural churches can obtain a seminary graduate as a full-time pastor. (An average attendance of 150 at Sunday morning worship usually is required to justify a full-time seminary graduate.)

Will this small rural church be willing to enter into a variety of changing arrangements, including some dependence on lay preachers, to secure the necessary ministerial leadership?

3. Rural America has been and continues to be one of the most rapidly changing frontiers of American society. These changes affect the role, the responsibilities, and the opportunities of the small rural church. This means new challenges to the leadership of the congregation.

Is the congregation willing to provide the opportunities for both the laymen and the pastor to participate in specialized inservice training programs? Is this provided for in the parish budget?

4. Rarely can the small rural church provide an adequate and comprehensive ministry to all of its members by itself. Usually the small rural church can offer Sunday morning worship, Sunday school, and perhaps one other programmed activity per week. Rarely can it by itself offer its members an adequate ministry to youth and young adults. Rarely can it alone offer its members the necessary variety of opportunities for involvement in ministry. Rarely can it offer by itself, for either old or new members, the desirable range of opportunities for personal and spiritual growth.

Is this small rural church willing to engage in cooperative efforts with other congregations in these areas of ministry?

5. Perhaps most important of all, most small rural churches still are training a significant number of children and youth who will be among the urban church leaders of tomorrow.

Is this small rural church training these children and youth to live in tomorrow's urbanized world and to be a part of the church of tomorrow? Or is it training them to live in the rural world of 1937 and to be a part of yesterday's small rural church?

The small rural church that can answer all five of these questions affirmatively probably not only has a will to live, but also has a reason for survival and is prepared to discuss with denominational representatives and leaders from other congregations some of the alternatives described earlier in this section.

It cannot be emphasized too strongly that these

193

questions and alternatives are not suggested as simply
a way of keeping small rural churches from closing.
That is not the goal!

These questions and alternatives are being suggested as possibilities for the agenda when concerned
Christians come together to talk about the future of
the small rural church. These alternatives are offered,
not as solutions in themselves, but as suggestions that
may stimulate the thinking of those who are concerned with a specific situation. These alternatives
are not offered as a means of maintaining the institutional life of every small congregation. In some cases
merger or dissolution may be more appropriate.

*These suggestions for a new agenda are offered on
the premise that in thousands of communities the
closing of the small church does represent a real loss.*
In these communities the closing of the church means
change by subtraction and the reduction of the ministry of the church. In these communities there is a
need for change by addition, by strengthening, reinforcing, and expanding the ministry of the Christian
church. In these communities there are people who
have not accepted Jesus Christ as Lord and Savior,
people who are self-centered rather than neighbor-
centered, people who have not realized the potential
that the Creator gave them, people who need the
ministry of the church and people who deserve the
opportunity to minister to others in the name of
Jesus Christ.

What's Ahead for "The Neighborhood Church"?

St. Andrew's Church was organized by a group of
members from First Church back in 1924, when the
City of Oakwood covered less than three square miles

and the population was slightly under 25,000. The man who developed this subdivision, on what was the far west side of the city in the 1920's, was a member of First Church and donated four 40' x 132' building lots for a new church. A parsonage was built on one of the lots and in 1928 a new church building was completed on the other three. The last of the indebtedness from that building program was finally paid off in 1944.

The 1970 census reported that Oakwood was just over the 70,000 mark in population and the city had grown to cover fourteen square miles. Instead of being the youngest of the three churches of the denomination in Oakwood as it was in 1924, St. Andrew's became the second oldest of the five congregations in that denomination when Calvary Church disbanded in 1965.

In 1952 the parsonage at St. Andrew's was converted into a parish hall. When that proved to be unsatisfactory, it was razed in 1956 and a new six-room church-school wing was constructed. This new addition also included a study for the pastor, a secretary's office, a church parlor that was paid for and furnished by the Women's Auxiliary, and a pair of modern restrooms. To everyone's surprise and joy, the twelve-year mortgage on this $85,000 project was paid off in 1964.

The neighborhood around St. Andrew's was comparatively stable until the mid-1950's. Several of the larger homes had been changed into two or three family structures back during the housing shortage of World War II, but to a substantial degree the neighborhood in 1954 was much like what it had been three decades earlier. In 1958, when the congregation celebrated the thirtieth anniversary of the con-

195

struction of their meeting place, it was noted that three of the houses in the same block with the church were still occupied by their original owners. The housing statistics from the 1970 census, however, revealed that over fifty percent of the residents within a five-block radius of the church had been living in their homes for less than four years. The median level of education for adults in that neighborhood was two years lower than it had been in 1960, the median age of all residents in the neighborhood had climbed from 32.7 in 1950 to 38.3 in 1960 and then dropped to 29.8 in 1970. Between 1960 and 1970 the number of widowed women in the neighborhood had nearly doubled. These statistics documented the comment of the city planning director who described that neighborhood as "filled with people who are either too young to stay or too old to move."

St. Andrew's Church reached its statistical peak in 1954 when the confirmed membership totaled 564, worship attendance averaged 235, the Sunday school attendance passed the 200 mark on 37 Sundays of that year and the receipts totaled $47,000 for all purposes.

This year worship attendance is averaging between 125 and 140, the Sunday school rarely has more than 80 persons in attendance, and one half of them are either in the adult classes or serving as teachers. The budget was set at $31,000 for the year, down $800 from last year's budget but still $1,300 above last year's actual receipts.

Last October a careful study was made of church attendance for four consecutive Sundays. It revealed a total of 263 different persons attended at least once. This total included 3 adult visitors, 11 children from non-member homes, 29 children of members, 19 members in the 14–21 age bracket and 201 adult members. This meant that 188 of the 408 persons carried on the membership roll did not attend even once in that four Sunday period. Only six of the seventeen remaining charter members attended at least once during October.

This attendance study also revealed that 91 of the 220 confirmed members who attended at least once in that month were age 65 or over, and another 67 were in the 50–64 age group. There were 34 members in attendance in the 30–49 age bracket—and only 4 of these lived within two miles of the church. Nearly two thirds of the 220 members who attended at least once in this period lived at least three miles from the church.

What is the future for this congregation?

Two years ago the thirty-one-year-old-grandson of one of the charter members suggested they consider a merger with either First Church or Bethany. His suggestion was overwhelmingly rejected. The sentiment of the majority could be summarized in the comment of one woman who argued, "The closest Protestant church to St. Andrew's is over three quarters of a mile away. If we closed, there would be no church left to serve this neighborhood."

Subsequently, a five-member committee was appointed to study how this congregation could serve the neighborhood more effectively. One part of the assignment was to discover what could be done to encourage newcomers to the neighborhood to attend St. Andrew's, or at least to send their children to the Sunday school at St. Andrew's. After three months the committee recommended the creation of a youth club for youngsters in their middle teens, with the comment, "It appears the adults are not interested in

197

a church like ours, but maybe we can reach the teen-agers." This was launched and met at the church every Friday evening, but was discontinued when the trustees complained about the damage to the property.

The fifty-three-year-old pastor of this congregation is in his seventh year at St. Andrew's and is making no secret of the fact that he is ready to move and probably will accept the first decent opportunity that comes along.

"These are good people," he commented when asked about the congregation. "They are loyal, most of those who live anywhere near here are faithful, they are good givers, and they love their church. The present church treasurer took office in 1951, he succeeded his father who served from 1924 until his son took over. That should give you some idea of the loyalty of these people to this church.

"Every one of the old members would give almost anything to see this church come back to the strength it had twenty years ago," continued the pastor. "While no one wants to talk about it, they know St. Andrew's is dying. They know that in another five or ten years they may not be able to afford their own full-time pastor. They saw what happened over at Calvary in 1965.

"But I guess most of them figure this church will be here until after they are dead and buried," he concluded sadly, "and then it will be someone else's responsibility."

What should this congregation do? What kind of program should be developed at St. Andrew's? What should the denominational leadership do?

The first comment that should be made in response to these questions is that it probably will not make much difference what any outsider suggests. During the past seven years denominational leaders have come in on three separate occasions and spent considerable time with the leaders of this congregation. There was no significant response to any of these consultations. The most active response came last fall with the attendance study. This was a direct response to a specific suggestion from a denominational staff person.

The second comment, and a more basic response to these questions, is to develop a frame of reference for looking at the St. Andrew's situation. In a book filled with brilliant insights, *Innovation in Marketing*, Theodore Levitt offers two comments that are relevant at this point. The first is that the organization that concentrates its energies on "pushing its product" tends to go out of business, while the organization that emphasizes a response to the needs of people has a tremendous future. The other is "unless you know where you're going, any road will take you there."

Today St. Andrew's Church clearly is "pushing its own product." Its product is a traditional ministry to the persons who have been members of this congregation for many years and to their children. This "product" does not arouse the interest of newcomers to the neighborhood. They are not interested in buying that "product" nor in helping to keep it on the market. They have no more interest in the continued availability of that product than they have in the continued availability in the market place of buggy whips.

To make suggestions about new programs that might be initiated at St. Andrew's also certainly would be a waste of time and effort *until* after the

199

members decide on purpose, role, and mission. Until the members decide where they are going, any program is as good—or as irrelevant—as any other. To prescribe programmatic suggestions before the congregation has determined what it is trying to do is as fruitful as giving highway directions to the driver who does not know his destination.

This same point also applies to the denominational representatives. Are they concerned about St. Andrew's because there is a church building of their denomination in this neighborhood? Or because they want to maintain "an outpost for ministry in this neighborhood"? Or because they are convinced there are unmet needs in this neighborhood and their denomination has the resources, the capability, and the responsibility to meet these needs?

A third comment that can be made about the situation at St. Andrew's is to recognize that today this is not a neighborhood church. It apparently was a neighborhood church during the three decades extending from 1924 to the mid-1950's, but it obviously is *not* a neighborhood church today. Therefore, an essential part of the process of planning for the future of this congregation must be to decide what it is today. When this has been done and when the congregation determines what its mission is in the days ahead, it will be possible to begin a potential discussion of program.

Most of the members of this congregation would strongly support the idea that St. Andrew's should concentrate on meeting the needs of people. But which people? The scattered and aging membership? Or the people moving into the neighborhood?

Some members will ask, "Why not both?" The

answer to that question is another question. Will the members at St. Andrew's willingly surrender control over the administration, the property, and the life style of that parish and accept the changes in life style and program that will be a part of the process of meeting the needs of the newcomers in the neighborhood? Very few long-established neighborhood congregations have been willing to do this.

This brings up the final comment about this congregation and illustrates one of the values of the use of this concept of categories or types in parish planning. Whenever a congregation changes from one type of parish to another type this almost invariably creates tensions and conflict within the congregation. It also means a change in role for the leadership, both paid and volunteer. This can be seen when Old First Church goes through the transition to become a metropolitan church, when the rural congregation becomes a suburban church as a result of the migration out from the city, or when St. Andrew's tries to make the change from a gathered congregation oriented to yesterday.

Usually this shift from one type to another type occurs unintentionally and gradually—as happened when St. Andrew's ceased to be a neighborhood church and became a gathered congregation.

Usually there also is a time lag between the reality of the situation and the perception of reality. This was illustrated very clearly at St. Andrew's when they built that new addition back in 1956. This was obviously planned by and for a congregation that identified itself as a neighborhood-oriented, three-generation family type church. It was actually constructed during a period when St. Andrew's was abandoning

201

that role and becoming a gathered one-generation type of parish.

What is the future for this congregation?

It appears to have two alternatives. One is to continue as a "chaplaincy" type gathered church with the primary emphasis on a "care" ministry to the members. After perhaps another decade or less in this role the remaining members could disband. The other alternative is to deliberately begin the process of changing to another type or role while the resources to do this are still available. There are no easy answers for congregations such as St. Andrew's.

The Marks of a Metropolitan Church

Of all the types of churches mentioned earlier, perhaps the most interesting, certainly one that represents a very high degree of specialization, and probably the one that usually has an impact all out of proportion to its size, is the metropolitan church. What is a metropolitan church?

Certainly one of the unique characteristics is that nearly every one of them began as some other type congregation, most often as a "First Church" type congregation. It should be emphasized, however, that the metropolitan church may or may not be located in the central business district. Most congregations with a downtown meeting place are not metropolitan churches, and several well-known metropolitan churches are located well beyond the central business district.

A metropolitan church may include many, many families, and it almost always has a comprehensive ministry to reach all members of the family, but it is

not a family centered church. The focus is *out* on the metropolis, not *in* on the member families.

Rarely will there be more than two or three metropolitan type congregations of a single denomination in any one metropolitan area, and in most there is no more than one. A list of the four or five hundred congregations in the United States that fit in this category would include Tabernacle Presbyterian Church in Indianapolis; The First Cumberland Presbyterian Church of Chattanooga; St. John's Episcopal Church in Jacksonville, Florida; Calvary Presbyterian Church in Cleveland; The First United Methodist Church of Peoria; The First Baptist Church of Seattle; The First United Methodist Church of Orlando; Holy Trinity Lutheran in Buffalo; The First United Methodist Church of Dallas; Luther Place Memorial Lutheran Church in Washington, D.C.; and Park Congregational Church (U.C.C.) in Grand Rapids.

After a decade of working with many congregations that either are metropolitan churches or are seeking that identity, it is possible to see several characteristics that distinguish the metropolitan church.

1. By definition, it is a nongeographical parish. The metropolitan church draws members from all parts of the metropolitan area.

2. Among the members and constituents there is not a major emphasis on a distinctive social class, cultural, ethnic, or racial identification. Persons from all compartments into which society is divided can be found within the metropolitan church.

3. The metropolitan church almost always has excellent preaching that attracts worshipers. This is both an asset and a distinctive mark of the metropolitan church.

203

4. The metropolitan church displays an aggressive interest in the social, political, and cultural issues that confront the people of the church in general, and the residents of the neighborhood in which the meeting place is located in particular. It also has an effective means of relating to laymen who feel compelled to respond as Christians to these issues. This includes both the *opportunity to discuss* these issues in the light of the Christian faith and traditions and the *opportunity to respond* in more active ways.

5. It has a dynamic evangelism program.

6. It has a systematic, varied, and redundant program for assimilating new members into the life and fellowship of the congregation. The metropolitan church is able to accept a high rate of turnover in the membership.

7. There is a balanced definition of purpose that includes a ministry to members, evangelism (an effort to Christianize the world), and witness and mission (an effort to humanize the world).

8. It provides both a ministry to members and varied opportunities for the members (and non-members) to respond to the challenge to minister to others in the name of Jesus Christ.

9. There is within the congregation, and in the community at large, a relatively clear understanding of the purpose(s) and mission this church has identified and of the reasons for its continued existence. (This does not mean that everyone will offer an identical response to a question on purpose and mission, but rather that a relatively large number of people will not have to hesitate and grope for an answer when confronted with such a question.) The metropolitan church is widely known and mention of the

name tends to provoke an image, not a blank, in the mind of the listener.

10. The metropolitan church places a very heavy emphasis on the importance of corporate worship.

11. It has an excellent ministry of music with a high rate of participation.

12. There is a major emphasis on celebration as an essential element in the life of the called-out community.

13. Among the members there is an acceptance—not simply a toleration—of diversity. The metropolitan church takes literally Romans 12:3-21 and I Corinthians 12:4-31.

14. There is an openness to innovation that is actually an expectation by members that their church will be on the frontier and will be a pioneer.

In addition to this openness, there also is a need for a high level of mutual trust among the members. Unfortunately, this is not present in all metropolitan churches.

15. It has a highly redundant system of communication to both members and to the residents of the entire metropolitan area, and a special effort is made to enhance two-way communication.

16. The metropolitan church values and respects tradition, and it recognizes the importance of tradition, but is not bound by tradition.

17. The orientation of the church, and especially of the leaders, is to today and tomorrow, not yesterday, but especially to today. The metropolitan church does not live in the past and it does not live only for the future. As much as any other type church, and more than most, the metropolitan church is a NOW church.

18. There is present a sense of excitement that is

felt by visitors and new members as well as by the leadership. The metropolitan church is, by definition, an exciting church.

19. The Christian education program not only emphasizes study, but also participation, involvement, response, and growth. It also includes several types of programming. In one class the emphasis—and attraction—may be the content, in another it may be the fellowship of the group, in a third it may be personal and spiritual growth, in a fourth it may be functional competence, and in a fifth it may be training in articulating the faith.

20. Almost invariably the metropolitan church has a strong and highly visible program for children and youth that attracts a large number of young persons from non-member households.

21. The metropolitan congregation places a very heavy emphasis on the role of the church as a reconciling agent in a fragmented and divided society. This is more important in the 1970's than ever before.

22. There is a recognition of the importance of place in the lives of people, and especially of older people. The metropolitan church understands that people need to be able to identify with a geographical and physical place.

23. The leadership uses carefully thought out criteria in making decisions. For example, "Will this course of action limit or increase the opportunities for participation?" or "Will this decision increase or reduce the degree of diversity in the life of this congregation?" or "How will non-members living in this neighborhood view this proposed course of action?" or "Will this enlarge or reduce our opportunities for ministry?" or "Is this a response to people's needs

or are we really only trying to sell our product?" In most cases ministry wins out over institutional maintenance in the allocation of resources in a metropolitan church.

24. The metropolitan church has a multiple staff, not all of whom need be full-time. It tends to rely more heavily on specialists than on generalists. It tends to employ more part-time persons than does the typical church with a multiple staff.

25. The metropolitan church averages at least 300 in worship on Sunday morning, and more likely averages 400 to 800.

26. The giving level averages at least $300 a year (and usually $400 to $500) times the average attendance at worship.

27. Consistently, year after year, the number of persons joining by profession of faith is greater than the number of members lost by death. When this comparison is made on an annual basis, two of the most important items are the trend and the number of times a minus figure appears.

The central point in interpreting this set of comparative statistics is to see these as a reflection of the church's appeal to persons in the 12-to-24 age bracket and to the parents of young persons age 12 to 16. Most persons joining a mainline Protestant church on profession of faith have a parent, a boy friend, a girl friend, or a spouse who already is a member of that congregation.

28. In the metropolitan church more people join by transfer (letter) than leave via the transfer route. This is especially useful as a quick index to see how newcomers view that church. The vast majority of adults joining a metropolitan church "shop" for a church home before making a decision. The church

in which transfers-out exceed transfers-in may be conveying a negative impression to visitors.

This is especially important today when a rapidly growing number of laymen are believing what many ministers have been preaching about, "the church is mission," and "the church does not exist for those in it, but for those outside it," and "the local church must be concerned about the community in which it is located." A great many laymen, including a large number who have not been active in any local church for years, believe this. They are "turned on" by the church that also appears to believe these statements. They are disappointed and turn away when they find a metropolitan church where these concerns are articulated but not practiced.

Today this group of people probably constitute the largest single group of potential new members for a metropolitan church.

29. The death rate in the metropolitan church tends to be above the denominational average. The metropolitan church of today often was a strongly family-oriented congregation ten or twenty or thirty or forty years ago. Instead of transferring their membership, however, many of these people continued as members. One result is an above average number of older members.

30. The leaders in metropolitan type congregations tend to be aware of a sharp distinction between witness and change. With its pluralism, diversity, and involvement, the emphasis in a metropolitan church tends to be on the church as a force for growth and change rather than on being a highly visible witness on specific issues.

31. While the definition of purpose in a metropolitan church tends to be expressed in broad terms,

it has been expressed, and the various elements of the total program and ministry are identified as part of the effort to fulfill that broadly defined statement of purpose. This tends to help members have a sense of direction and feel a sense of progress.

32. Perhaps most important of all of the marks of the metropolitan church is a confident belief in the power of the Holy Spirit and a sense of obedience to God.

This is an extensive, but an exhaustive, list. Not every metropolitan church displays every one of these characteristics, and there may be other important distinguishing characteristics that are not on this list.

Conclusion

"We are trying to develop a plan for this congregation for 1985," announced the president of the church council at St. Timothy's Church as he called to order the first meeting of that parish's long-range planning committee. "This committee has two tasks. The first is to determine what this congregation should be and what our ministry should be in 1985. The second is to determine how we get from where we are now to where we should be in 1985."

This committee would facilitate its work if it would add a third task to this list and place that at the top of the agenda. That task would be to determine what that congregation is today. Regardless of how carefully and thoroughly this committee develops plans for the ideal church of 1985, they will have difficulty describing a way to get from here to there unless they know where they are today. Identifying the type of parish their congregation is today is one approach to this task.

SUGGESTIONS FOR FURTHER READING

Bailey, Wilfred M. and McElvaney, William K. *Christ's Suburban Body*. Nashville: Abingdon Press, 1970.

Beckhard, Richard. *Organization Development: Strategies and Models*. Reading, Mass.: Addison-Wesley Publishing Co., 1969.

Brewer, Earl D. C. *et al*. *Protestant Parish*. Atlanta: Communicative Arts Press, 1967.

Douglass, H. Paul. *1000 City Churches*. New York: George H. Doran, 1926.

Festinger, Leon *et al*. *Social Pressures in Informal Groups*. Stanford: Stanford University Press, 1963.

Fisher, Wallace E. *From Tradition to Mission*. Nashville: Abingdon Press, 1965.

Fray, Harold R. *Conflict and Change in the Church*. Philadelphia: Pilgrim Press, 1969.

Gans, Herbert J. *The Urban Villagers*. New York: The Free Press, 1962.

Judy, Marvin T. *The Cooperative Parish*. Nashville: Abingdon Press, 1967.

Levitt, Theodore. *Innovation in Marketing*. New York: McGraw-Hill, 1962.

Obenhaus, Victor. *The Church and Faith in Mid-America*. Philadelphia: Westminster Press, 1963.

Schaller, Lyle E. *The Local Church Looks to the Future*. Nashville: Abingdon Press, 1968.

Shippey, Frederick A. *Protestantism in Suburban Life*. Nashville: Abingdon Press, 1964.

Trexler, Edgar R. *Ways to Wake Up Your Church*. Philadelphia: Fortress Press, 1969.

Winkel, Gary H. "The Nervous Affair Between Behavior Scientists and Designers." *Psychology Today*, March 1970.

7
THE MOST
NEGLECTED TASK

"This is a dying church," Dr. George E. Sweazey is reported to have told a pre-assembly conference on evangelism at the General Assembly of the United Presbyterian Church in the U.S.A. In making this statement the former moderator cited a membership decline of 56,000 and a decrease of over 100,000 in Sunday school enrollment figures for his denomination in one year. Similar statistical decreases have been reported in several other denominations in recent years.

This is only one item in the array of evidence that suggests evangelism is the most neglected task as the typical parish plans for its mission. The same pattern is revealed in parish after parish that adopts the concept of program budgeting described in chapter 2. The typical congregation spends between sixty and ninety percent of its money on a ministry to members. It is not unusual to find a congregation allocating twenty to forty percent of its budget to witness and mission. It is very unusual, however, to find a congregation allocating as much as four percent of its budget to evangelism.

On the other hand, however, scores of churchmen and many local churches have taken a new look at this task and their experiences may be of value to the parish that takes seriously its responsibilities in evangelism.

Before reviewing a few of these lessons from experience, one basic point deserves emphasis. There has been a temptation in many parishes to put all of the evangelism eggs in one basket. In one the leaders depend entirely on revivals, in another the members contend that social action and evangelism are two sides of the same coin, in a third the pastor argues that evangelistic preaching is the only effective tool, and in a fourth the people believe the Sunday school is the best evangelistic program. In today's pluralistic society the congregation with an effective evangelistic program almost always has several elements in this package. Five of these may be of interest to parish leaders who take seriously the Great Commandment in the twenty-eighth chapter of the Gospel of Matthew.

Why Do People Join a Church?

Before looking at these, however, it may be helpful to review why the people who are members of a local church say they are members of that congregation today. There have been scores of surveys directed to this question and, while the methodology and questions asked show considerable variation, the results fall into the same basic pattern. In a national sampling of members of the United Church of Christ, for example, four out of ten members declared the denominational label was a "very important" reason for joining that church. This response is typical of the results from other studies. Depending in part on the denomination and in part on the format of the questionnaire, between one third and one half of most church members indicate that denominational loyalty was the critical factor in why they belong to the congregation of which they are now members.

The other major consideration was a contact with a person (parent, spouse, boy friend, girl friend, pastor, neighbor, or church visitor) who invited the individual to join. Depending somewhat on the format of the survey and the conditions under which it was conducted, most studies report thirty-five to sixty percent of the respondents identify a personal contact as the primary reason for belonging to the congregation of which they are now members.

Far down the list of why people join a particular congregation are location, the program, the building, and newspaper advertisements. While it still accounts for only a small proportion of all church members, a factor that appears to be growing in importance is the response of the person who says, "I joined this congregation because it is doing what I believe the Lord is calling the church to do and to be today."

What does this mean?

In simple terms this means that the typical congregation is largely dependent on two factors for reaching people beyond the membership. One is the person of that denomination who chooses a new church primarily out of denominational loyalty. He may simply walk in, or he may be attracted by the ministry or witness of a particular congregation of his denomination, or he may be especially receptive to an invitation.

The other factor is the person-to-person contact, usually along friendship or kinship lines, with non-

213

members. This brings up what is still the most popular and probably the second most effective single approach to evangelism today.

Visitation Evangelism

Every year literally thousands and thousands of local churches plan a "calling program" to contact the unchurched residents living in the neighborhood around the church building. Frequently the greatest effort is devoted to recruiting a corps of "volunteers" to call. All too often this turns out to be a sterile, somewhat embarrassing, and uncreative experience for everyone involved. Occasionally this becomes one of the most important and vital experiences of the year for two or three dozen individuals.

Why was this a creative and inspiring experience in one parish and a dull and wearisome routine in another? In a great many congregations the answer to this question can be summed up in one word—training.

The Rev. H. Thomas Walker, who has trained hundreds of laymen in visitation evangelism, suggests there are five essential elements in an effective program of visitation evangelism. First, the visitor has to have a faith to proclaim and know how to articulate it. Second, the visitor has to believe and express confidence in the church as the body of Jesus Christ. Third, he has to possess and express concern for the person he is visiting. Fourth, he has to be able to reveal or share his own experience of faith. Fifth, he has to be able and willing to help the person he is visiting make a response to the challenge of the Christian gospel.

The parish that is contemplating a program of

visitation evangelism probably will have a better experience if the visitors are trained before they are asked to call and if the training program deals with all five of these issues.

In one congregation where this was done the pastor was asked to evaluate it. "The second most important benefit from this program," he replied, "was that we initiated an effective contact with over two dozen people who previously had no meaningful relationship with any church. The most important benefit, however, was what happened to the lives and spiritual vitality of the fifteen laymen who shared in the training and calling experience."

A Presbyterian Church of Canada congregation used a somewhat similar approach. The leaders decided to try to reach everyone in the community with the gospel. The first step they took in implementing this decision was to call together a group of members for a series of discussions in which each individual told what his faith meant to him. Each one was enriched by the experiences of the others. Each learned how to articulate his faith in his own words. Then, but not until then, they went out calling on the unchurched people in the community. Each visitor had something to say and knew how to say it.

Ours or Theirs?

During the past decade hundreds of congregations have proved that it is very difficult to recruit new members on the premise that they are needed to maintain that congregation's life and program. People appear to have no interest in simply maintaining someone else's organization.

Recognizing this fact of life, what appears to be a

215

growing number of local churches have initiated the creation of what some critics describe as "congregations within a congregation." They have stopped saying (by actions), "Come join our church and support the program we have planned and have implemented. After you have proved your loyalty by a few years of regular participation we may let you join the in-group." These congregations have started to say (by both word and deed), "How can we meet your needs? Give us a clue and we will help you plan and implement the programmatic response that meets your needs; but we will be glad to help rather than control."

This approach has been especially fruitful in bridging the age or cultural gap that separates some congregations from a large number of persons who live in the neighborhood of the meeting place. Perhaps the clearest evidence that this gap exists and is difficult to overcome is the large number of congregations that have left behind their old meeting place as a result of merger, relocation, or dissolution. They took this drastic step with great reluctance and only because they were convinced "Nobody can reach the people moving into this neighborhood, they simply aren't interested in the church!" Subsequently, a new congregation was organized that began to use the old building. Sometimes it was organized by the same denomination and sometimes by a different church group from the residents of that neighborhood, and it soon was larger than the congregation that had vacated the building. To some cynical outsiders it appeared that the old congregation had erred in its evaluation. The people moving into the neighborhood were not opposed to the church, they simply were not interested in a local church of the style and with the type of control represented by what they perceived in this long-established congregation.

What Are Your Needs?

A related approach that has become the central theme in the evangelistic outreach of a growing number of church groups can be summarized in one sentence. The church must be responsive to the needs of people. Since this is also an essential element in the central thesis of this book, this is not the only place the reader will encounter this point of view. The reason for introducing it again in this chapter is that it appears to be the most effective approach to evangelism in use in the churches today. The Rev. Reynold N. Johnson of the Lutheran Church in America describes this as the "new face of evangelism." He says "The new face is that you start with the person's interests and hopes rather than your desire to win a member. Unless you show him this kind of concern, he will find it difficult to believe that a relationship with Christ will transform him."

This approach requires a local church to recognize that different people have different needs, that the same person may have different needs at different times and that the Christian faith enables the church to offer a unique response to people's needs. It has been demonstrated over and over that the congregation that is sensitive to the needs of people is able to establish a meaningful relationship with people outside the church. This relationship becomes the foundation for proclaiming the Good News. What is basically the same general pattern can be seen in wealthy suburban neighborhoods, in the inner city, in rural communities with a dwindling population, in county seat towns, and in stable middle-class neighborhoods. The greatest barrier to this approach to evangelism is *not* represented in the frequently articulated question, "But how do we identify the needs to which we should be responding?" The biggest barrier is the normal, natural, institutional pressure to subvert all efforts to identify and respond to people's needs to maintenance of the organization.

A Difference in Styles

A fourth approach, which overlaps the last two mentioned, perhaps can best be described in the single word "style." This approach is based on two assumptions. First, people are different from one another. Second, every local church has its own style of ministry; an individual may view the style of one congregation as bland and unappealing while he sees the style of another to be exciting and attractive.

Both of these assumptions are being rejected by many leaders in several denominations who apparently are acting on the assumption that all local churches are the same all over and all people are the same everywhere. These leaders appear to be interested in reducing the number of different points of contact between people outside the church and a worshiping congregation by reducing the number and variety of local churches.

In the more affirmative approach, these assumptions on differences are taken seriously. This can be seen most clearly in the parish that adopts for itself a distinctive style of ministry, recognizing that this distinctive style will have significant meaning to some people while others may be "turned off" by that particular style. The people in that congregation are able to live with that mixed response, however, because they do not view themselves as the only Christian congregation in the world or God's only instrument for reaching people with the gospel.

In very simple terms, this approach to evangelism is based on an affirmative acceptance of diversity and pluralism.

The Reaffirmation of Membership

Perhaps the most neglected dimension of this most neglected task of the parish is the assimilation of new members, especially those who join on profession of faith or by confirmation, into the life and fellowship of the worshiping congregation. The congregations in the dozen largest mainline Protestant denominations in the United States "drop from the rolls" by action of the governing body of the congregation over 700,000 names each year. A disproportionately large number of these are the names of individuals who joined *that* congregation by profession of faith, or confirmation, or believer's baptism, and either lapsed into inactivity or disappeared from view.

As they recognize the seriousness of the issue, many congregations are placing as much emphasis on this as on the original contact with non-members. The variety of responses is illustrated by these examples. Since the transfer of a person's membership to another congregation by letter apparently is in fact a very important reaffirmation of membership, some congregations are lifting up the transfer as a major celebration rather than treating it as simply a part of the paperwork routine. In other congregations each member is asked to come forward and publicy reaffirm his membership vows annually. Another re-

219

sponse is to establish a probationary membership-category which is a required preliminary step before achieving full membership. A fourth approach is to develop clearly stated expectations of the responsibilities of membership in that congregation in operational terms. This has the apparent effect of sharply reducing the proportion of new members who lapse into inactivity.

In these and similar approaches evangelism is viewed as more than simply a method of adding names to a membership roll. It is seen as a process that provides the opportunity for an individual to affirm his faith in Jesus Christ as Lord and Savior, and to reaffirm that faith in a variety of ways on subsequent occasions.

SUGGESTIONS FOR FURTHER READING

Mumma, Howard E. *Take It to the People.* New York: World Publishing Co., 1969.

Schultz, Hans Jürgen. *Conversion to the World.* New York: Charles Scribner's Sons, 1967.

Trueblood, D. Elton. *The Company of the Committed.* New York: Harper & Row, 1961.

8
ECONOMY OR PERFORMANCE?

The careful reader may have noticed that one of the characteristics of the literary style of this book is redundancy. There is considerable repetition. For example, the same point about the importance of good preaching was made in chapter 4 and repeated twice in chapter 6. On at least a half dozen occasions the same suggestion, phrase, or sentence is used in two or three different sections. A careful editor could have reduced the length of this book to 180 pages or less by eliminating every instance of repetition.

The specific goal in writing this book, however, was not to produce a tightly written volume with no repetition or redundancy. The goal in writing this book was to transmit a message from the author to the reader. Therefore, the primary criterion in evaluating the style cannot be summarized in the question, is this a tightly written volume with no repetition or redundancy? The primary criterion for evaluating the literary style can be summarized in one question, however. Did the message get through?

The literary style of this book illustrates one of the two or three most critical issues in parish planning and church administration. That issue can be stated in a simple question. Which is the more influential force in the planning and decision-making process, the desire for efficiency and economy or maximizing the effectiveness of the organization in fulfilling its purpose? These often are incompatible goals. This point can be illustrated by looking first at the subject of communication.

The sale price of this book could have been reduced by eliminating all repetition and duplication. It would cost less to manufacture a 160- or 176-page book and a lower price tag could have been placed on the volume.

The cost of achieving this goal of economy would have been poorer communication between the author and the reader. Much that is written is misunderstood. As was pointed out in chapter 5, many messages that are sent are never received and many that are received were never sent. The letters to the editor of the newspaper or magazine reveal only the tip of this iceberg. If the length of this book had been reduced one third by editing out all the redundant words and phrases, the selling price could have been reduced, but the chances that the reader either would misunderstand or fail to receive the message the author is sending would increase at least tenfold.

In recent years specialists in information theory have discovered that brevity and clarity often are incompatible goals. This should not be regarded as a startling new discovery. Years ago, before use of the long distance telephone became so widespread, it was not uncommon for a telegram to be sent which closed with the words, "letter following."

In verbal communication redundancy is a means of reducing the probability that the message that is being communicated will be distorted, misunderstood, or filled with error. The more important the message, the greater the emphasis on redundancy.

Thus over nine tenths of the words and phrases used in the communication between the pilot of an airplane and a control tower operator are redundant. In the typical sermon about sixty percent of what is said is redundant, but this figure may rise to eighty or ninety percent when the preacher is attempting to drive home a key point or his central thesis. While it has been impossible to check the basic data, it appears that the degree of redundancy reaches the ninety-eight or ninety-nine percent level in the communication of courtship. This again illustrates the central point here—the more important the message, the greater the degree of redundancy.

The world in which I live is filled with redundancy. The car I drive has a redundant deceleration operation; the manufacturer calls it a dual brake system. The seminary with which I am affiliated has a system of administration, instruction, and concern for students that is filled with redundancy. The churches I visit and work with are parts of an extraordinarily redundant ecclesiastical system. The individual congregations duplicate each other's programs and ministries, they overlap one another both geographically and functionally, they are extravagant in the use of manpower, and they are anything but models of economy and efficiency.

Redundancy is certainly one of the key words to be used in describing the assortment of newspapers, magazines, journals, and books that come into our house every month. Redundancy is a major characteristic of the messages that come into our household via radio, television, our children, and our friends and neighbors.

To a large extent my life is governed by the actions of a redundant two-house national legislature, a re-

223

dundant two-house state legislature, and a series of overlapping units of local government.

Redundancy—or duplication, inefficiency, repetition, overlap, and extravagance, if you prefer those words—is a characteristic of the public school system our children attend, of the network of retail stores at which my wife shops, of the range of choices open to me in buying gasoline for our automobile, and of the air transportation service available to anyone in the Chicago area interested in flying to New York or Cleveland or Los Angeles or Dallas.

One of the outstanding examples of redundancy in our era has been the Apollo series of spacecraft. Apollo 11, which first carried two men to the moon, was an example of this. The spacecraft and the entire operation was filled with a series of redundant systems. The overlap, duplication, extravagance, repetition, and excess components were widely discussed in July 1968. The value of redundancy in a spacecraft was shown far more dramatically with Apollo 13 in April 1970.

During the past dozen years there has emerged a theory of redundancy which has direct application to the fields of church planning and administration. The source of this new knowledge is largely information theory, systems analysis, organizational theory, and, more recently, public administration.

The Essential Characteristics of Redundancy

In applying redundancy theory to church administration there are three points that merit emphasis. First, redundancy is not simply a safety measure. It is that—the dual brake system on an automobile or the emergency electrical system in a hospital are examples of redundancy as safety measures. It is much more than that, however; safety is but one expression of the value of redundancy. Redundancy basically is a means of both suppressing error and of eliminating the undesirable effects when error does occur.

Second, the theory of redundancy replaces the traditional approach to the elimination of error with a new frame of reference. Traditionally the goal has been to achieve perfection in each component of a system and thus produce an error-free system. In a paper published in 1956, John Von Neumann introduced the idea that an organization can be developed which is more reliable, or free of the effects of error, than any of its parts by adding sufficient redundancy. To put it in technical terms, the probability of failure in an organization (system) decreases exponentially as redundancy factors are increased.*

A third important element in redundancy theory is that the duplicate systems must be independent of one another so that a failure in one will not automatically trigger a failure in another. In considering the implications of this point it is important to distinguish between overlap and duplication. While both are forms of redundancy, they are different types of redundancy and the rules that apply to one do not necessarily apply to the other. Overlap is useful in suppressing error within a single system.

* The essence of Von Neumann's theory is expressed in this sentence, "By using large enough bundles of lines, any desired degree of accuracy (as small a probability of malfunction of the ultimate output of the network as desired) can be obtained with a multiplexed automation." "Probabilistic Logics and the Synthesis of Reliable Organizations from Unreliable Components," in C. E. Shannon and J. McCarthy, eds. *Automata Studies* (Princeton: Princeton University Press, 1956).

225

A New Frame of Reference

Application of the theory of redundancy to church planning and church administration requires acceptance of a new frame of reference for the planner and the administrator. Professional church leaders have tended to view zero redundancy as a highly desirable goal. This is a natural product of a culture in which the twin gods of efficiency and economy have been objects of widespread adoration.

A common expression of this efficiency-economy orientation is illustrated by a comment such as this. "In this community there are 900 residents and five churches. There is widespread duplication of effort and of program. They overlap each other in dozens of ways. Only two of them have enough members to constitute a minimally efficient operation or to provide the range of program and ministry that a church should offer today. Everyone would be better off if, instead of being so badly overchurched, this place had only one or two congregations. Think of the money that could be saved if we only had to heat one building in the winter instead of five, and if we were paying the salary and providing housing for only one minister instead of five! Think of the time and energy of laymen that could be saved if we needed only one church treasurer instead of five, one Sunday school superintendent instead of five, and one governing board instead of five!"

Does this sound familiar? Logical? Rational?

How about this one? "Our denomination has seven major program boards—education, evangelism, social action, missions, stewardship and finance, women's work, and lay life and work. Once each one concentrated on its own special area of concern; in recent years, however, each one has begun to overlap the work of two or three others. Today there is a tremendous duplication of effort and it is impossible to coordinate their programs. Every one of them is sponsoring training programs for both laymen and ministers. Why can't they get together and develop one training program that will include all of their concerns and emphases?"

Does this sound familiar? Logical? Rational?

Both of these illustrations reveal an orientation toward efficiency and economy or zero redundancy.

Both represent a widespread dissatisfaction with the duplication of effort and the wasteful functional overlap that characterizes the institution and organizations of American Protestantism.

Both of these sets of comments would be described by redundancy theorists as irrational responses to duplication and overlap.

To understand why redundancy theorists would classify comments such as these as irrational it is necessary to shift to a new frame of reference in looking at religious organizations.

In this new frame of reference all Christian religious organizations—congregations, denominational agencies, interchurch organizations, *et al.*, are viewed as one extremely large, very complicated, and imperfect information system. The task of this system or network of religious organizations is to communicate the Good News. This is a much more complex task than it first appears and requires the execution of a very large number of different operations. It requires continuous communication, not only between those within the system (church members) and those outside the system (non-members), but also the transmission of information from one part of

227

the system to other parts of the system. In fact, most of the effort in this system is directed at the *internal* transmission of information.

When viewed from this perspective it quickly becomes apparent that the reduction of error in the transmission of information and the carrying out of responsibilities becomes a basic objective of the total operation. The traditional approach to this objective has been to make each component of the entire system a perfect and error-free operation. The objective of zero defects and zero redundancy is an expression of this approach.

If, however, Von Neumann's thesis that increasing the degree of redundancy increases the reliability of the system is accepted, then it is possible to accept more easily the assumption that the system always will have many components that are functioning improperly, inadequately, or not at all. If it is accepted as a fact of life that distortion or error may enter at any point in the system at any time and if Von Neumann's thesis is accepted, then it is logical to place the primary emphasis, not on creating a perfect and error-free system with zero redundancy, but on improving the quality of performance of the system and reducing the seriousness of error in any one part of the system. From this frame of reference the goal of zero redundancy can be described as inconsistent, self-defeating, or irrational.

An excellent illustration of the application of the theory of redundancy in church administration can be seen in scores of northern cities in the parish system of the Roman Catholic Church during the past one hundred years. The city first is seen as being divided into a series of geographical parishes. There is no geographical overlap among these parishes. On top of this layer of geographical parishes there were several layers of nongeographical parishes serving various language and ethnic groups. Thus the residents of a single neighborhood might be served by six or eight parishes, the geographical parish plus a parish for Czechs, one for Poles, one for Germans, one for Slovaks, one for Italians, one for Ukranians, one for Slovenes, and one for Hungarians. Duplication, overlap, and repetition were widespread, but the emphasis was not on efficiency nor minimizing unit costs, but on getting the message through.

From this perspective the obvious objective is not in the direction of zero redundancy, but rather in the direction of optimum redundancy. This means a shift in emphasis from reducing costs by seeking to eliminate redundancy to allocating resources in a manner that will increase redundancy to the optimum level.

Problems in Acceptance

How rapidly and how widely will the theory of redundancy be accepted by churchmen? Where will it have its greatest impact? What will be the consequences?

There are a number of reasons why questions such as these are difficult to answer. First, it is comparatively difficult for people to accept and adopt an idea that requires a change in their perspective or in the way they view the world. It is much easier to gain acceptance for a new idea or practice that is compatible with the traditional frame of reference and with the accepted criteria for decision-making.

Furthermore, the theory of redundancy will encounter considerable opposition because it tends to support many of the patterns and practices which characterize the contemporary religious scene, but which have been under vigorous attack for several years. In the churches, as in the rest of society, there is a sharp contrast between practice and preachment. In business, in government, in all types of voluntary and nonprofit operations the twin goals of efficiency and economy are widely articulated while the theory of redundancy often describes actual practices. This has been going on for so long that it will be very difficult for many people to deny the folk wisdom behind their words and to begin to defend their actions.

Possibly the biggest barrier to widespread application of the theory of redundancy is that it requires a change in the orientation of the leadership in the churches. In marketing terms this means focusing on the needs of the customer rather than on the product that is being sold. In educational terms it means focusing attention on the needs of the student rather than on the convenience of the administration and faculty. The railroads ran into trouble when they became railroad-oriented rather than transportation-oriented. The film companies in Hollywood almost were put out of business by television because for too many years they saw themselves in the movie business rather than the entertainment business.

In local church terms this problem of orientation is illustrated by the comment: "We have an outstanding worship service at eleven o'clock every Sunday. We worship in a beautiful sanctuary. The music is superb. The preaching is the best in the city. But each Sunday two thirds of our members stay away. How can we get them to attend this superb worship service?" The problem can be stated very simply. Is this parish trying to meet the needs of people in worship or are the leaders concentrating on selling "their" product?

Application of the theory of redundancy tends to force a change from an orientation to the institution and its needs to an orientation to the task that is to be performed. Instead of focusing on the worship service and its attractive features, the emphasis should be on the need to which worship is a response and to needs of the people who are staying away.

A fourth factor that will make it difficult to gain popular support for the deliberate application of this theory is semantic. Many of the words that are associated with the theory have value-laden connotations. The list includes the word redundancy itself as well as duplication, overlap, repetition, and extravagance. This problem is intensified by the fact that the theory undercuts a concept which can best be expressed by the words economy and efficiency, both of which have a very attractive and positive ring.

Since it is going to be extremely difficult to gain adherents to a theory of decision-making that is built on such negative terms as repetition, duplication of effort, and overlap of function, and which is in opposition to such hallowed terms as economy and efficiency, the logical next step is to revise the terminology. Two attractive and feasible possibilities are performance and pluralism. Neither one has any serious built-in handicaps; both have a moderately attractive ring and both fit the situation.

From the frame of reference described earlier, performance is a good word to describe what people in the churches should be concerned about as they evaluate this network of religious institutions and organizations. It is a much better term to use as the basis for evaluation than such value-laden words as efficiency, economy, duplication, overlap, or extravagance. Hopefully it will focus attention on the end rather than encourage the error of identifying the means as the end. Too often church leaders have become so enamored with the means or the objectives or the strategy (economy, efficiency, joint use of buildings, church mergers and unions, a new building, shared staff, computers, cooperative purchasing, etc.), that these become ends in themselves, thus replacing the original goals of the organization.

Pluralism is a very attractive word, not only for describing the religious scene in contemporary America, but also for describing the nature of the organizational system that is encouraged by application of the theory of redundancy.

If the semantic problem can be avoided and if the confusion between ends and means can be eliminated, it is reasonable to expect that redundancy theory will have a major impact on the decision-making process in American Protestantism during the next dozen years.

This proposal that the emphasis in church administration should be on performance rather than on eliminating duplication of effort and on minimizing unit costs can be supported by an examination of the practices in the public schools. In more precise terms, Raymond Callahan has suggested that the appropriate question for school administrators should not be "How can we operate our school?" but rather should be, "How can we provide an excellent education for our children?" The reader should have no difficulty in translating these questions into church administration or church-planning terms.

In support of his argument Callahan has described

how the cult of efficiency affected school administration. For four decades following the popularization of "scientific management" by Frederick W. Taylor in 1910–1911, professional school administrators tended to emphasize "efficiency," "unit costs," "economy," and "lowest costs" rather than the quality of the educational program.

As a result of this emphasis on scientific management, several methods were devised to test the efficiency of a school system. One was to measure the number of hours each room in a school was being used each year. Another was based on the fact that each year a child was in school cost the taxpayers a certain sum of money. Therefore an "efficient" school would be able to report that the investment of this sum of money resulted in one child advancing one grade. Thus each year the efficiency of the school system could be measured by comparing the number of pupils who received a double promotion or skipped a grade with the number that were forced to repeat a grade. Optimum efficiency was obtained when these two numbers were equal. This, according to the cult of efficiency, indicated that the taxpayers got a dollar's worth of educational achievement for each dollar spent!

The most serious consequence of this emphasis on efficiency is that the goals of the entire system often are subverted by the yardsticks used to measure efficiency. If the "efficiency" of the system is determined by the number of hours that the building is used each week, the natural response of the efficiency-conscious or approval-seeking administrator is to seek to increase the number of hours the building is in use each week. If the classroom teacher is judged on the basis of the number of pupils who are made to

233

repeat the grade and the number who receive double promotions, this probably will force that teacher to redefine the classroom goals accordingly. This diverts attention from questions about the quality of what is happening in the building when it is in use. This kind of emphasis on efficiency can be worse than silly, it can adversely affect quality and performance.

Redundancy and Criteria

If the theory of redundancy is taken seriously, where will the impact be felt in the churches?

The initial impact will be seen in the frame of reference used in evaluating the programs, organizations, and goals of the churches. This can be illustrated by suggesting some of the questions that grow out of an application of redundancy theory.

Should the desire of each national board to publish its own newsletter or magazine be viewed as duplicating the responsibilities and the jurisdiction of the national denominational magazine, or perhaps as a subtle step in empire-building? Or should it be seen as a natural response to the desire of the board to make sure *its* message gets through?

Did the resistance to comity and to other efforts to coordinate the new church development programs of several denominations indicate a lack of interest in interchurch cooperation? Or was it a natural response by each denomination to the desire to make sure *its* message got through to the people in each community?

In evaluating the program and work of each national board in a denomination, should the emphasis be on drawing strict lines of demarcation separating the functions of one agency from those of all other agencies in the interests of eliminating duplication and overlap? Or should some degree of overlap be accepted as necessary in order to make sure the responsibility is fulfilled? If so, what is the point of optimum redundancy?

Should the pastor who receives three letters in the same mail from three different church agencies publicizing training opportunities be irritated by this duplication and waste? Or should he view this as an attempt by each agency to make sure *its* message got through?

Should the proposal in the local church to shift from one to two worship services on Sunday morning be viewed as wasteful duplication since the combined attendance can be accommodated very easily at one service? Or should this proposal be discussed as an attempt to make sure the message gets through to more people?

Should the proposal to unite the 500-member former Methodist church with the 350-member former Evangelical United Brethren congregation that meets in a building three blocks away be viewed as an effort to eliminate duplication of effort and reduce unit costs now that the two denominations have united to form The United Methodist Church? Or should the proposal for merger be examined in terms of the theory of redundancy as well as in terms of efficiency and economy?

Does redundancy theory have anything to say to the proposal to merge the 80-member open country congregation with the 400-member congregation in town?

The pastors in nine of the fourteen churches in a county-seat city formed a ministerial association. When they discussed a ministry to the municipal

235

hospital, four favored a system whereby each minister would serve as chaplain for one week on a rotating basis. Two wanted to hire a retired minister to serve as a part-time chaplain. Three wanted each minister to develop a corps of lay visitors from among his members and not have anyone serve as the chaplain. Does the theory of redundancy offer a frame of reference or any criteria for deciding this question?

A theological seminary has four men who teach in the field of biblical studies. Should two offer courses only in Old Testament and two offer courses only in New Testament? Does the theory of redundancy shed any light on this question?

Does redundancy theory provide a framework for discussing the number, geographical location, and denominational affiliation of theological seminaries?

A Lutheran congregation owns a parcel of land next to a Presbyterian church. The Presbyterians have completed their building program and hold two worship services with a combined average attendance of 300 each Sunday morning in a $190,000 sanctuary that can seat 375 including the balcony. Should the Lutherans build their own separate worship facility or should they try to work out a cooperative arrangement to use the Presbyterian's sanctuary? What criteria should they use in making this decision?

In a large midwestern city the Presbyterians are sponsoring the development of a two-year-old, new, nongeographical, racially integrated congregation that is attracting people from all sections of the metropolitan area. Should the Episcopalians go ahead with the proposal of one of their clergymen to sponsor a similar congregation? What are the criteria to be used in making this decision?

The Barriers to Acceptance

This brief list of questions illustrates several of the difficulties that await those who want to apply redundancy theory to church planning and church administration.

The most obvious one is that while most people will find it easy and comfortable to discuss redundancy theory in general terms, when it comes to the direct application in specific situations life will become more difficult. As was pointed out earlier, redundancy theory suggests that the application of the conventional yardsticks of efficiency and economy often may be an irrational approach to the problem. Many people will find this to be extremely threatening. If you cannot depend on efficiency and economy as acceptable criteria for decision-making, on what can you depend?

A second obstacle is that application of redundancy theory may be interpreted as legitimatizing a unilateral and noncooperative approach to church planning and church administration. This, of course, is nonsense. The only problem here is for those who oppose all forms of pluralism and who favor a unitary approach to the institutional expression of the church. Their problem, however, is with the concept of pluralism rather than with redundancy theory. Redundancy theory simply offers a new frame of reference for examining the alternative solutions to a specific problem and in the development of a set of criteria for choosing from among the alternatives. If taken seriously, redundancy theory should encourage inter-church cooperation in planning and administration. It encourages an acceptance of pluralism and the use of a frame of reference from which all components of the religious scene are viewed as parts of a single system, rather than as completely separate and isolated operations.

A more serious problem is that since redundancy theory emphasizes performance, application of the theory requires agreement in two areas where it is very difficult to secure agreement. The first is in the definition of purpose, the formulation of goals, and the ordering of priorities.

What is the optimum degree of redundancy in designing a spacecraft for a trip to the moon? The engineers want to maximize the probability that the round trip will be completed safely. They favor a high level of redundancy. The scientists want to send more scientific equipment along and therefore favor a lower level of redundancy in the design of the spacecraft in order to allocate more space for equipment. If the astronauts have the decisive voice, of course they will favor optimum redundancy!

At St. Paul's Church one person places a high value on maximizing the opportunities for people to participate in corporate worship. He favors three worship services each Sunday morning. Another person places a high value on Christian education and wants to allocate two hours of the Sunday morning schedule solely to Christian education. What is the optimum degree of redundancy in planning the Sunday morning worship schedule in that parish?

The other place in which it is difficult to get agreement is on the criteria to be used in determining the optimum degree of redundancy. Presumably this means the use of criteria that reflect purpose and can be used to measure performance. Most of the criteria used by church leaders today, however, are useful in evaluating means, but of little value in measuring performance. This means that new criteria for measuring performance must be developed. It also means that many of the old and widely used criteria that are related to efficiency and economy (means) must be discarded and replaced by the new ones that are designed to measure performance (ends). (See chapter 4 for a more extended discussion of this point.)

A fourth problem, and possibly the most serious of all, is that application of this concept is vulnerable to the perils of excess. If three churches in one neighborhood means that more people are likely to be reached with the Good News than if there is only one church, why not plan for sixty congregations?

The answer is that the goal should be neither zero redundancy nor maximum possible redundancy. The goal is the optimum level of redundancy. A strong case can be made on behalf of the concept of a two-house legislature. It is much more difficult to develop a persuasive argument in favor of a thirteen-house legislature.

What is the optimum level of redundancy? How is it determined? What are the criteria? Those are the critical questions. They must be answered. In developing answers to these questions it should be remembered that the optimum level of redundancy varies with the importance of the subject, with the quantity of available resources, and with the time. Application of cost-benefit evaluation techniques, of probability theory, and of insights borrowed from information theory, systems analysis, and operations research will be useful in developing answers.

For the person who rarely drives at night it probably is worth the additional cost to have a dual brake system on his car, but it would not be worth the

239

added cost to have two systems for illuminating the highway in front of the automobile. A national denominational department of social action may be able to justify having its own monthly periodical, but it would have greater difficulty in persuading people that it needed to publish two magazines in order to get its message through.

While these and similar questions and problems are important, they should not obscure the most important potential contribution of redundancy theory to church planning and church administration. This is the shift in perspective that focuses attention on the quality of performance rather than on the economics of operating the system. As people in the parish begin to plan for tomorrow, and as they reflect on the value of emphasizing the concepts symbolized by such terms as purpose, pluralism, goals, policies, diversity, self-evaluation, program planning, and innovation, they might be well advised to consider replacing the word *economy* with the term *redundancy*.

SUGGESTIONS FOR FURTHER READING

Callahan, Raymond E. *Education and the Cult of Efficiency*. Chicago: University of Chicago Press, 1962.

Landau, Martin. "Redundancy, Rationality, and the Problem of Duplication and Overlap." *Public Administration Review*, July/August 1969.

Levitt, Theodore. *Innovation in Marketing*. New York: McGraw-Hill, 1962.

Pierce, J. R. *Symbols, Signals and Noise*. New York: Harper & Row, 1961.

Schaller, Lyle E. "Interdenominational Church Planning." *Planning for Protestantism in Urban America*. Nashville: Abingdon Press, 1965.